CONTENDING
for the
HEART

———◆◆◆◆◆———

THE HIDDEN KEY TO
YOUR CHILD'S BEHAVIOR

BY

JIM ERTEL

Harrison House
Tulsa, OK

Scripture quotations are from *The New King James Version* of the
Bible unless otherwise noted. Copyright © 1979, 1980, 1982, Thomas
Nelson, Inc.

Scripture quotations are marked KJV are taken from *The King James
Version* of the Bible

Webster's New World College Dictionary, 3rd Ed. New York: Simon &
Schuster, Inc., 1996.

15 14 13 12 11 10   9 8 7 6 5 4 3 2

ISBN 13: 978-160683-011-6
ISBN 10: 1-60683-011-2
Copyright © 2010 by by James Ertel
P.O. Box 2063
Monument, CO 80132

Published by Harrison House Publishers
P.O. Box 35035
Tulsa, Oklahoma 74153
www.harrisonhouse.com

Contents

In Loving Memory
of
Raymond Simpson
October 20, 1920 – March 13, 2000

Man of God

Faithful Husband

Loving Father

An example to all who knew him in life
The father of my bride
The finest man I have ever known

Thank You

First, thank you to my lovely wife, Shirley. She is and has been my best friend and confidant for over four decades. Together, by the grace of God, we have raised a family and weathered many storms. I will forever be thankful to God for Shirley, and for the love, joy and peace that she brings to me and our family.

To my friend, Andrew Wommack, thank you for writing the foreword of this book. Those heartfelt words mean more to me than I could ever express. And thank you for your life's message of God's unconditional love and grace. It has changed my life and given me a more clear understanding in applying that message to the family. I will always be grateful.

To Stephen Bransford, a master wordsmith and story teller; thank you for your encouragement and friendship. What you have taught me, in our many conversations about writing, has had a profound influence on this book. Everyone should read at least one of your novels, especially *"The Last Photograph."*

Thank you, Wendy Francisco. You have been the perfect editor. Your sincere belief in the message of this book has made all the difference. And you knew just how to help without completely destroying my ego. Congratulations on your new illustrated book, *GoD and DoG*.

I would also like to thank my publisher, Harrison House, for bringing this book to the market. Their excellent staff has taken a personal interest in the success of this book. Never tiring of my questions, they have given me the most professional service and personal attention that any author could ever want.

Foreword

I have known Jim and Shirley Ertel from a distance for decades. But it has been my pleasure to have them on my staff since 2004. During that time I've seen firsthand how they interact with others and I'm pleased to say they live what they preach. I've been in their home and have met their children and grandchildren and they have fruit that testifies to the truths in this book.

As Jim brings out in this book, no one on their deathbed wishes they had worked more or had accumulated more things. Failures in relationships are always our biggest regret. I don't believe this is accidental. We have an enemy going about seeking to destroy relationships with those we love the most.

There is an all-out assault against the family. Friction between parents and children is intensified today by a world that doesn't support traditional moral values. Parents are often overwhelmed and feel helpless.

In this book, Jim uses an easy-to-read narrative

style to communicate fundamental Bible truths, just as Jesus did. These stories will touch your heart, inspire you, and convict you as they did me when I read them.

Jamie and I have had more problems with our children than most parents. I've often prayed and sought the Lord about what I could have done differently and I've received more insight from Jim's book than any other I've read on the subject.

In my case, it wasn't an issue of a lack of love or effort. I gave parenting everything I had. But as with everything in life, good intentions are not enough. There are right and wrong ways of doing things. I believe Jim has hit upon the core of raising godly children.

As you read this book, let the Holy Spirit reveal these truths to you. Resist the tendency of pride that would only have you focus on what is wrong with your children and let the Lord speak to you about your own heart. We can't fix in others what is broken in ourselves.

I pray the Lord would touch your heart as you read this book and contend for the heart of your child.

Andrew Wommack

Chapter 1

You're Making a Big Mistake

Cindy waved as she pulled into the driveway. She could see her mother peering through the small window in the front door anxiously awaiting their arrival. Before she had time to turn off the engine and unbuckle the seat belt, her mom had covered the distance from the porch to her car, had the back door open, and was reaching for April in the car seat. "I've got her. I'll meet you inside, Cindy."

"Good morning to you too, Mom," said Cindy. Grandma was enjoying every minute of babysitting her first grandchild. April was six months old and her captivating smile could melt anyone's heart, but Mommy was still the only one who could make her laugh out loud.

Every day it was becoming a little more difficult for Cindy to kiss her little girl goodbye and head for work. She was acutely aware of how fast April was changing. She would be crawling soon and in a few more months, taking her first steps.

"Well, I better get going or I'll be late for work. See you tonight, Mom. Call me if April needs anything."

What will I miss today? Cindy thought, walking back to the car. She watched as Grandma made her way to the living room next to the picture window holding Baby April. While she buckled her seat belt and started the motor, Grandma was helping April wave goodbye. Tears filled Cindy's eyes as she drove away. "Thank you Lord that we have someone we can trust to love and care for our daughter," she whispered, and then after a short pause, "but shouldn't that someone be me?"

She had a very good job: executive secretary for the Dean of Business at the university. She was well respected, the benefits were great, and they needed her income, especially if they expected to qualify for a home loan. Her friends thought she had it made: a good husband, a great job, and a built-in babysitter just a few blocks away. What could be better?

You're Making a Big Mistake

While Cindy was pregnant, she and her husband, Mike, had excitedly planned for April's arrival. Those plans included Grandma doing the babysitting while they were at work. But now that April was actually here, they were discovering a love for their child far beyond what they could have imagined. Both Mike and Cindy were now having second thoughts about that decision.

That evening at dinner Cindy began telling Mike what had happened at Grandma's house. "Mom told me that April was trying to crawl today." As Cindy continued the report he could see the disappointment in her eyes and hear the longing in her voice. This had to change, and he knew it.

"I'm not sure how it will all work out Honey, but we have talked about this long enough, I think you should give your two week notice tomorrow."

"Really?"

"Yes, really."

"But how will we ever get out of this tiny apartment and buy our house, and what about our old car?"

By now, Mike had learned to read between the lines when Cindy asked a question in that way. He knew she wasn't talking about a new house or better car. She wanted to quit work and was hoping for his support.

"I don't know about all that, but I do know that our daughter needs you. April doesn't care if we own a big house or drive a new car. You and I are the ones who want those things."

As much as Cindy would have liked to have her own home, those words were exactly what she needed to hear. More than anything, she wanted to be the one to see April take her first step and to hear her speak her first words.

The next morning she felt excited and fearful; excited about the prospect of staying home with her daughter, but a little afraid of how her boss would react. Mr. Williams was a forceful and persuasive man who would not take her resignation lightly. She drove to work early and placed the letter on Mr. Williams' desk. Two minutes after he arrived, he called her in.

"You can't resign," blurted Mr. Williams as he threw the resignation letter back across his desk to her. "I need you. You're the only one who knows what's going on around here."

"I'm sorry Mr. Williams, but Mike and I have made the decision."

"Well, it's the wrong one," he said insistently, "and what about that home you and Mike were planning to buy? You'd better reconsider. At least take the weekend to think it over, OK?"

"Well all right, but it won't change our decision." With that, Mr. Williams motioned for Cindy to leave his office. He didn't speak to her for the rest of the day.

Saturday morning, Mike and Cindy were finishing a late breakfast when the door bell rang. Cindy got up to see who it was.

"Well hello, Mr. Williams, this is a surprise."

"I was wondering if I could speak with you and Mike for a few minutes."

"Well, I guess so. Come on in and have a seat. I'll get him."

"Who's at the door?" Mike asked.

"It's my boss. He wants to talk to us."

"Good morning Mr. Williams," Mike said as he reached to shake his hand, "What brings you to our house this morning?"

"Mike, I want to talk to you about Cindy's resignation. I think the two of you are making a big mistake. Cindy is walking away from a great career opportunity and I really need her. So, I would like to make her an offer I think will interest both of you. Cindy, I'm willing to give you a thirty percent raise in salary and make your work schedule a little more flexible for April's sake. I think you should know that I have never done this for anyone before. This is a very generous offer and I promise you, I won't be making it again. So what will it be?" he demanded.

Mike didn't hesitate for a moment. "Well, it is a good offer Mr. Williams, but Cindy and I are going to stick with our decision."

Mr. Williams shook his head in disbelief, stood up and walked out without saying another word. "Well, that was interesting," Mike said, "but we are doing the right thing, Cindy."

Mike and Cindy are a great example of a couple who realized they had nearly been caught in the web of materialism. A nicer home with a big mortgage, a newer car they couldn't really afford, a few more credit card bills, and then Cindy's resignation would not have been an option.

Many of their friends and even some in their family thought they had made a big mistake and that it made no financial sense. However, it was one of the most important decisions they would ever make. It was a choice to sacrifice their own wants and desires for the sake of their children. And it was a decision that they would revisit many times.

I wish I could say that it all worked out perfectly. But, over the next ten years, they faced many financial struggles, any one of which would have been solved by Cindy returning to the work force. But she didn't. They had adopted a new perspective. Instead of looking at things from their own point of view, they began to look at things from the point of view of their children. April and her little brother, Taylor, who arrived three years later, never knew which of their clothes came from Goodwill, K-Mart or Baby Gap, and they didn't care. All they knew was that they were thoroughly loved by Mommy and Daddy.

Mike and Cindy are a great example of a couple who realized they had nearly been caught in the web of materialism.

Unlike many parents, Mike and Cindy were unwilling to out-source their responsibility and leave the development of their children's character to others. No matter who those people may be, the children's pastor or youth leader, the soccer coach or the day care worker, none of them will ever love and care for a child like a parent. John 10:12-13 says, *"But a hireling, he who is not the shepherd, one who does not own the sheep, sees the wolf coming and leaves the sheep and flees; and the wolf catches the sheep and scatters them. The hireling flees because he is a hireling and does not care about the sheep."*

Parents are not hirelings. God views their relationship to their children in the same way that He views Jesus'relationship to the Church. They are shepherds of the heart, who have been given the responsibility, the authority, and the power to protect their children from the one who comes to steal, kill, and destroy. Like Jesus, they lead their children to abundant life.

Proverbs 22:6 says, *"Train up a child in the way he should go, and when he is old he will not depart from it."*

The word *old* there is not referring to age. It means mature. Maturity is not necessarily a function of age. I have seen, as you have, twelve-year-olds who are more mature than some thirty-year-olds. Maturity is a function of teaching and training, not age. God has promised us if we will train our children that we will get the results we are looking for. Mike and Cindy believed that promise and accepted the responsibility.

It takes time, effort and self sacrifice to fulfill that scripture. How many times have you heard a parent say, "I'm too busy to spend a lot of time with my kids, so I make the time we spend together quality time." For many parents, quality time is often nothing more than activity and entertainment and Mom is reduced to the transportation director. The whole idea of quality time is a justification for the lack of time spent interacting with our children. The truth is that the quality times we all desire are only found within a great quantity of time. They usually come unexpectedly in brief moments hidden within seemingly unimportant activities. And when they come, the door to the heart is open allowing you to impact your child in a powerful way.

I remember one special night with my son. He was seven at the time. We had spent the afternoon and evening with our kids at Grandma and Grandpa's house. It was late but a beautiful night for a walk. We only lived a few blocks away so I asked Shirley

The whole idea of quality time is a justification for the lack of time spent interacting with our children. The truth is that the quality times we all desire are only found within a great quantity of time.

if she would drive home with our daughter, Jill, while Jeremy and I walked. The two of us held hands as we headed home.

"How was school today?" I asked.

"Good," he replied.

"Recess is really the best time, huh?"

"It's OK."

I was a little surprised by his answer so I continued. "You have fun playing with the other kids, don't you?"

"I usually play by myself."

"Why is that?"

"I don't think they like me."

This was not the time for me to get analytical and attempt to solve the problem. His heart was exposed and he was looking for me to comfort him. "You know what Jeremy?"

"What?"

"If I were there, I'd spend the whole recess playing with you; I'll always be your friend." That was enough to make him smile. I would call that an unexpected quality moment.

Mike and Cindy determined that their children were their number one priority. It was costly, but the end result was worth it. By the time their children were teenagers, their financial position had completely turned around. And neither Mike nor Cindy could recall a time during those years of having a tight budget that their children ever felt they had missed out on anything. They both smile as they talk about the great relationship they now have

The opportunities that you provide and the things that you give to your children do not make up for your personal time and attention.

with their children because of the sacrifice. Sadly, this has become the exception rather than the rule. Parents, knowingly or unknowingly, often sacrifice their children on the altars of the cares of this world, the lust of the flesh and the deceitfulness of riches. (Mark 4:10.)

Somehow, the enemy has duped us into believing that love is measured by the ability to provide our children with all the world's goods and unlimited opportunity. There is certainly nothing wrong with things and opportunities, but in the end that is not what children really want. They want YOU. The opportunities that you provide and the things that you give to your children do not make up for your personal time and attention.

Recent findings in a poll conducted by Associated Press/MTV of people ages 13-24 reveals that they were the most happy when they spent time with their family and loved ones. This poll was not directed at Christians but taken from a cross section of the population. It found that family really matters to young people. Parents are seen overwhelmingly as a positive influence in their lives. Nearly half said that one of their parents is their hero. Money and the things money can buy were almost never mentioned as a source of happiness. These answers were even a surprise to MTV.

To win the heart of your children, you must begin early and that means you need to find a way to be there. Obviously, there are many families, especially ones headed by single moms, who have fewer options. They would love to have a grandmother, an aunt, a close friend, or someone else they could trust to love and care for their children, but it is not always possible. Many feel they have no choice but to work and place their children in daycare. For those in this situation, I encourage you to pray and ask God for a creative solution. Don't give up or lose hope. The Bible is full of great examples and stories of ordinary, imperfect people who emerge from difficult situations to accomplish great things.

Proverbs 22:6 places no restrictions or qualifications on its promise. It may be more difficult in your situation, but not impossible. In Mark 10:27, Jesus said, *"With men it is impossible, but not with God: for with God all things are possible."* And 1 Corinthians 13:8 says, *"Love never fails..."* Love your children, lead them to Jesus, and then watch the Holy Spirit make a way when there seems to be no way. God is faithful to His Word.

In the next chapter, you will read a story about a young couple that understood how important it was to go beyond discipline and impact the heart of their young daughter. They knew the difference between punishment and correction, and applied that knowledge. If you have had questions about using corporal punishment to correct your children, this next story may help.

Contending for the Heart

Discussions Questions
Chapter 1
You're Making a Big Mistake

1. How was parenting modeled for you, and what are you planning to do differently?

2. What fears, worries, or concerns do you have about parenting?

3. Do you think it is possible for both parents to have a career and also do a good job raising their children? Why or why not?

4. If both parents are working, what can you do to ensure your child's needs are being met— physically, emotionally, and spiritually?

5. What are your goals as a parent? How do you think knowing the outcome you are striving for might help you fulfill your role as a parent?

6. Are you willing to make personal sacrifices of time and priorities for your children? Can you think of a situation where what you desire and what is best for your child might be in conflict?

7. Where would your rank your personal desires and ambitions in comparison to your children's needs?

8. How do you express love to your children?

9. What are some ways to make sure you are giving enough personal time and attention to your child?

Chapter 2

Strong Willed Redhead

Ron and Debbie enjoyed entertaining their close friends and this Saturday evening couldn't have been a more pleasant time to fire up the grill. By five o'clock everyone had arrived with kids in tow and with their favorite desserts in hand.

Debbie soon found herself weaving her way through the family room and stepping over children on her way to the deck where Ron was manning the grill. He loved wearing that tall white chef's hat and colorful, "My Dad's the Best Dad" apron.

As he brushed the ribs with barbecue sauce, Ron's buddies began to press him for his secret. "Come on, tell us what's in the sauce." Ron was known for the best ribs in the neighborhood. But as usual, He refused to disclose his personal, top secret, *I could tell you but then I would have to kill you,* barbecue sauce recipe.

By mid-evening everyone had eaten far more than they should have. They made their way to the family room where they settled in for dessert, coffee, and conversation. The kids, always wanting to be in the middle of everything, were already there along with all the toys from the toy box downstairs. Watching them play was great entertainment and it gave the parents an opportunity to share stories and compare notes.

"The Broncos play San Diego tomorrow," Ron said to a buddy, while watching Lisa, their strong willed three-year-old, out of the corner of his eye. Although they didn't believe the old wives tale about feisty redheads, she seemed to be living up to the reputation.

One by one she passed each adult, looking at them with her mischievous smile. Target identified, she swung, hitting one of the women on her exposed knee with a hard toy.

"Ouch!"

Then, Lisa calmly stepped away and turned around to see if Daddy was looking. His expression assured her he hadn't missed a thing.

Oh no, not now, Ron thought. *I really wish I could just ignore it this time.* But he knew what Lisa was thinking. She was sure she had Daddy over a barrel; he wouldn't do anything with all these people around. Ron and Debbie had been working diligently at correcting Lisa's behavior, especially the desire she had developed recently to hit people. They had agreed that nothing would be allowed to slide. Ron knew what he had to do.

"Lisa, come here to Daddy." He glanced quickly at Debbie and obviously she had seen what happened too. "Lisa, you know better than to hit. Give me the toy and go tell Mrs. Adams you're sorry."

"No!" she exclaimed. The response was definite and it was loud. Lisa had just raised the stakes. In a room that had been abuzz moments before, you could hear a pin drop. Ron and Debbie had always been considered good parents with great kids and now everyone was waiting to see how they would handle this very public challenge.

Without hesitation, he picked Lisa up, excused himself, and carried her to the bedroom upstairs. They both knew this routine well and Lisa had already begun to cry. Ron sat down on the edge of the bed, turned Lisa around, and looked her straight in the eye.

"Lisa, you know I don't want to, but I am going to have to give you a spanking. Do you know why?" She looked away. "Look at my eyes Lisa," he said. "We have told you not to hit because it hurts people. If you had said I'm sorry to Mrs. Adams, we wouldn't be up here now. Instead, you told me no."

The light wooden spoon was always handy. It would sting but did little more. Most of the time Ron had to hold Lisa firmly over his knee or over the edge of the bed; she seldom submitted to spankings willingly. Three firm swats, then he stood her up. "Look at my eyes Lisa." Her eyes spoke louder than words, revealing the attitude of the heart. "Are you ready to go down stairs and say you're sorry?"

Crying hard, she screamed, "No" All he had really succeeded at doing was making her mad.

Lisa's determination to win the battle of wills had only increased. Ron knew this was going to be a long session. He continued the pattern; each time he gave her three swats, made her look him in the eyes, and then asked the question again. He was looking for something very specific. Ron and Debbie understood that spanking was not a matter of punishment. It was not a price to be paid for breaking the rules. Ron was looking for a change of heart.

There was a knock at the bedroom door. "How are things going?" Debbie asked quietly. "You've been up here for a long time."

"We're making progress," he replied. "I'll be back down as soon as I can."

Little by little, Lisa's attitude began to change. Finally, when he asked the question for what seemed like the eleventh time, she broke into tears. These were no longer tears of pain and anger but genuine tears of sorrow. This was the response of a changed heart. She reached to him with open arms, "I'm sorry Daddy."

Ron also began to weep, as compassion and love filled his heart. He lifted Lisa to his lap and held her close. "I love you," he whispered as he gently stroked her head. She clung to him tightly and sobbed, not wanting to let go.

He needed to get back to their guests, but Ron realized the significance of what was taking place and the power of forgiveness and reconciliation. This was one of those important moments and he couldn't afford to waste it. It was an opportunity to speak into Lisa's life. Her heart was now like a sponge, ready to receive. So for the next fifteen minutes or so, he spoke softly about how much God loved her and how much Mommy and Daddy loved her. When he sensed she had received all she could, he ended the conversation as he always had. "Sweetie, you're a good girl, now act like it, OK?"

"OK Daddy, can I go play now?"

"Yes, if you tell Mrs. Adams you're sorry."

"OK."

Lisa hit the floor running ready to join back in the fun. A quick stop to say "I'm sorry" and she was playing again as if nothing had happened. Ron listened for her apology to Mrs. Adams and then, exhausted from the ordeal, leaned back on the bed and sighed. *How many more of these sessions will it take?* he thought. *This wears me out.*

Ron and Debbie understood a very important issue. In fact it may be the most important issue of all when correcting the behavior of your children. A spanking should never be used as a punishment, but rather as a tool to bring about a change of heart. Proverbs 4:23 says, *"Keep your heart with all diligence, For out of it spring the issues of life."*

> *Ron and Debbie understood that spanking was not a matter of punishment. It was not a price to be paid for breaking the rules.*

The word "issues" here also means boundaries or borders. Ron and Debbie realized that if they could help Lisa establish the boundaries within her heart, in time correct behavior would follow naturally.

The goal here was never to make Lisa regret her behavior because of the consequence that followed; the scripture says that this produces death, not life.

In 2 Corinthians 7:9-10 we read:

Now I rejoice, not that you were made sorry, but that your sorrow led to repentance. For you were made sorry in a godly manner, that you might suffer loss from us in nothing. For godly sorrow produces repentance leading to salvation, not to be regretted; but the sorrow of the world produces death.

The goal here was never to make Lisa regret her behavior because of the consequence that followed; the scripture says that this produces death, not life. As the Apostle Paul wrote, godly sorrow leads to repentance. Then, when genuine repentance occurs, reconciliation can take place. In those sweet moments of reconciliation come great opportunities to mold the heart. Each time we correct our child's behavior without bringing them to repentance, we have simply punished them. That causes the heart to harden, little by little, making it even more difficult to soften and shape the next time.

In truth, spanking should be an act of love. That is why it is so important not to correct your child while you are angry. Anger wants to punish, to exact some degree of pain and suffering equal to the offense. Love, however, is not a response to a provocation, but seeks to correct for the benefit of the one being corrected. In 1 Corinthians 13:5-8, we read *"(love) does not seek its own, is not provoked, thinks no evil; does not rejoice in iniquity, but rejoices in the truth; bears all things, believes all things, hopes all things, endures all things. Love never fails."*

Proverbs 13:24 says, *"He who spares his rod hates his son, But he who loves him disciplines him promptly."* Proverbs 23:13-14 says, *"Do not withhold correction from a child, For if you beat him with a rod, he will not die. You shall beat him with a rod, and deliver his soul from hell."* This is a very strong statement, one that many would rather ignore. Is it possible that a parent who refuses to discipline his son or daughter really hates them? According to scriptures, if words mean anything, that's a true statement. The question is: Do we believe the Word of God or the words of our modern day psychologists who claim that spanking creates angry and violent children?

That verse also says that we are to discipline promptly. If we will, it accomplishes two important things. First, the behavior is changed and peace is restored in the home. Second, the more important of the two, it relieves your child of guilt. When children break your rules, their conscience convicts them, creating turmoil in their heart. Leaving that to fester and build is not love. It causes our children to ignore their conscience and harden their heart.

Is it possible that a parent who refuses to discipline his son or daughter really hates them?

As you read in this story, after Lisa had been corrected and reconciliation had taken place, she ran off and played as though nothing had happened. She was happy, free of guilt and self condemnation. In the Old Testament, under the Law, a clear conscience was achieved through the shed blood of an animal sacrifice. It foreshadowed the day when Jesus would sacrifice His blood once for all and reconcile the entire world to God. The reason for the spanking was to bring Lisa to a point of reconciliation with her parents. It foreshadows the relationship she will one day have with Jesus. Such discipline is uncomfortable and difficult, but real love demands confrontation. The fruit is well worth the effort.

Proverbs 23:13-14 tells us that when we correct our children and use the rod in the process we will deliver their souls from hell. There is no other way to interpret this; it is talking about the use of corporal punishment in correcting our children. However, the word "rod" spoken about in this scripture actually means stick, switch, or branch. It isn't talking about finding a tire iron to beat your child; it's simply talking about what we refer to today as a spanking.

They understood something else, and that was when to spank.

Ron and Debbie chose to believe Scripture. They had experienced the fruit of its application many times. They understood something else, and that was when to spank. When Lisa hit Mrs. Adams, all Ron initially asked her for was an apology. It wasn't until she screamed "No," defying Ron's authority in an overt act of rebellion that he had to take the next step. He knew that rebellion could destroy Lisa's life and future.

The best example of this may be the story of King Saul in 1 Samuel 15. God promised Saul a kingdom that would last from generation to generation. But Saul allowed rebellion and stubbornness to enter his life, and eventually lost that promised kingdom to David. It took a few years for the results of his rebellious act to become apparent, but just as Samuel said that he would, he lost everything and died in disgrace.

> *So Samuel said: "Has the LORD as great delight in burnt offerings and sacrifices, as in obeying the voice of the LORD? Behold, to obey is better than sacrifice, and to heed than the fat of rams. For rebellion is as the sin of witchcraft, and stubbornness is as iniquity and idolatry. Because you have rejected the word of the LORD, he also has rejected you from being king.*
>
> *1 Samuel 15:22-23*

When little children rebel, it is usually nothing more than a simple challenge to your authority as a parent. Their own self-centeredness and selfishness are at the root of the problem. They have no idea that you have their best interest in mind. At this stage it must be confronted as Ron and Debbie did in this story. The result was a changed heart that produced the fruit of changed behavior. However, if rebellion is not confronted while children are young it will manifest in their life as an adult, and as we learned in the story of King Saul, the consequences can be devastating.

I have been writing about spanking as a means of changing the heart and correcting behavior. However, as our children grow older, spanking must come to an end and we must make a major transition in the way we deal with their hearts. In the next chapter you will read a story about a little boy and his mother who are experiencing that transition.

Discussions Questions
Chapter 2
Strong Willed Redhead

1. Do you think that setting boundaries for your children is important? What are some boundaries you have set for your children?

2. What beliefs do you have about disciplining your son or daughter? Do you have any fears or concerns in this area?

3. How do you deal with rebellion and stubbornness?

4. As the need arises, how will you demonstrate forgiveness and reconciliation to your child?

5. What opportunities have you found to speak into your child's life?

6. What are some things you would like to say to your child? What do you want to make sure he or she knows about their identity?

7. What are some ways you have found to reach the heart of your child?

Chapter 3

A Change of Heart

"Michael James," Ann always called him by that name when she was serious, and now she had had enough of his bad behavior. "That's it, go to your bedroom right this minute. You're in big trouble." When Mikey heard her use that name he knew he was in jeopardy of getting a spanking. And when followed by, "Go to your bedroom," it left little doubt.

Mikey really was a good boy; usually kind to his brother and sister and obedient to Mom and Dad. At nine years of age he was the oldest of the three children. Being the older of the two boys, he naturally assumed the role of the alpha male and from time to time felt the need to reinforce the social order. This was one of those occasions.

Taylor, his little brother, was crying again because Mikey had jerked the Wii game controller from his hand for the third time. He then proceeded to push him aside and play the game by himself. Frustrated, Ann looked at him from across the room and gave it one more try.

"Mikey, give the controller back to your brother." He acted like he didn't hear her. That was his last chance, the next thing he heard was his proper Christian name spoken with authority, "Michael James." Off to the bedroom he went, mumbling something along the way, probably to prepare himself for the inevitable.

Ann took a few moments and had another sip of coffee before following him to his room. The Lord had been speaking to her about not over reacting when her children were disobedient and making sure that she did not discipline while angry. Once calmed, she grabbed the dreaded wooden spoon and headed upstairs. What happened next surprised her.

As she reached for the handle to open the door of Mikey's room she suddenly stopped. She could hear him talking and decided to wait for a moment and listen. "Jesus, I'm sorry," he said sweetly. "I know I shouldn't treat my brother that way. Please forgive me, I won't do it anymore." After hearing those words, she just stood there quietly. She could feel the lump in her throat as tears began streaming down her cheeks. She realized the significance of what she had just heard. "I'm so thankful, Lord, that I didn't barge in while I was angry and miss this opportunity," she whispered.

Mikey had just made a major transition in his life. Of his own free will, he was acknowledging his sin, asking for forgiveness, and repenting of the behavior. It was obvious to Ann from his sincerity that this was not an attempt to avoid discipline. He had no idea that she was listening. It was a heartfelt prayer to Jesus; and maybe for the first time, he really understood that he was accountable to someone far greater than Mom and Dad.

Standing there quietly, Ann remembered something that had happened just a few months earlier. *Could it have been the turning point?* she thought. Ron, Ann's husband, had been seeking a way to help their children understand the grace of God. He had spoken with a good friend who made a suggestion that had been effective with his kids and Ron thought it was a great idea. He planned to give it a try when the opportunity presented itself.

He didn't have to wait long. Mikey once again acted in a rebellious way and found himself waiting in the bedroom for Dad. To his surprise, Mom and Dad came into his room together. That almost never happened.

"Mikey," Ron began. "You know why we're here, right?"

"Yeah, a spanking."

"And you know how Mommy and Daddy are always telling you that Jesus died for our sins and that he took our punishment?"

"Yeah."

"Well, I want to show you what that really means. Mommy is going to give me the spanking that you deserve."

Ron knelt down and leaned over the edge of the bed. Ann moved next to him where she stood with the wooden spoon. The reality of what was about to happen gripped Mikey's heart.

"No Daddy! No Daddy," he shouted, "I'm supposed to get the spanking."

"I know, but I'll take it for you this time." Ann then proceeded to give Ron three swats as Mikey broke into a full cry.

"I'm sorry! I'm sorry," he shouted while trying to

grab the spoon from her hand. "I won't do it again Mommy, please don't spank Daddy anymore."

After the three swats, Ron sat back on the floor. Mikey was obviously shaken, not knowing what to do. With love and compassion in his eyes, Ron looked at his little boy and reached to him with open arms, "I love you Mikey." Before he could finish what he wanted to say, Mikey was in his lap hugging him with all his might. "I love you," he repeated. "But I want you to know that Jesus loves you even more."

Maybe that made more of an impact than I imagined, Ann thought.

Regaining her composure, she gave a little knock on the door and walked in. Mikey turned to look, expecting the worst.

"Mikey, I was listening outside your door and heard you praying to Jesus."

"You did?" he said shyly.

"Yes, I did, and I want you to know that I'm proud of you and I know that Daddy will be too when I tell him. I was going to give you a spanking. You know you deserve it. But because of what I just heard there's no need." Immediately, the sad look on Mikey's face transformed into a smile.

The heart change she always looked for when correcting Mikey had taken place without her intervention. Ann realized that the days of using a spanking to change his behavior may have come to an end. Mikey was making the transition from the law to grace.

This is a great example of the application of the spirit of the law instead of the letter of the law. 2 Corinthians 3:6 says, *"Who also made us sufficient as ministers of the new covenant, not of the letter but of the Spirit; for the letter kills, but the Spirit gives life."* If Ann would have barged in, determined to administer a spanking, it would have amounted to nothing more than punishment. It would have left Mikey confused about what Mom and Dad really wanted. And it would have continued to build a performance mentality that only leads to disappointment and self-condemnation. He needed to know that his relationship with Mom and Dad wasn't dependent on how well he kept their rules.

> *He needed to know that his relationship with Mom and Dad wasn't dependent on how well he kept their rules.*

To understand why this was so significant to Ann and her husband, you must first understand the philosophy behind it. A philosophy can be used like a road map; it gives you a starting point and a destination with mile markers along the way to mark your progress. Unfortunately, few parents have ever thought about their philosophy. When they are asked, "Where are you leading your children and why are you leading them there?" the answers are usually something like: "I want them to be happy and loved," "I want them to have a good education," or " I want them to be healthy and safe." Some forward thinking parents might even say, "I want them to have a real purpose in life." All are reasonable and valid desires, but they are simply desired outcomes without any specific direction to reaching them.

In the next few pages I will introduce a biblical Christian philosophy for raising children that I believe can help guide you as a parent. I want to emphasize "biblical" because there are many humanistic philosophies being promoted today. They often sound very good, even logical, but in the end they lead to failure because they are rooted in humanism and not in the Word of God.

Humanism can be defined as a system of thought rooted in human-based morality, without regard for the existence of God and His Word. 1 Corinthians 1:20,25 says, *"Where is the wise? Where is the scribe? Where is the disputer of this age? Has not God made foolish the wisdom of this world? Because the foolishness of God is wiser than men, and the weakness of God is stronger than men."* In 1 Corinthians 3:19 and 20: *"For the wisdom of this world is foolishness with God...The LORD knows the thoughts of the wise, that they are futile."*

Colossians 2:8 says this, *"Beware lest anyone cheat you through philosophy and empty deceit, according to the tradition of men, according to the basic principles of the world, and not according to Christ."*

The philosophy I'm writing about is according to Christ. It is not a formula or a methodology and it doesn't offer "how-to's" for every possible situation you might face. Raising children is not an equation to be solved or an exact science to be understood, it's an art. You are the artist and the heart of your child is the canvas. God has given you the power and the authority to paint an image on their hearts and you are always at work with a brush in hand. Whether you know it or not, your words, actions, and deeds are painting an image on your child's heart every day. It's an image of God and who they are in relation to Him.

Will your children see God as a harsh taskmaster, a keeper of the law? Will they see Him as a God of tolerance, indifferent to their behavior? Or will they see Him as a loving Father who wants to guide, guard and govern in their best interest? You're the artist, it's up to you.

The Road Map

Everything that God created on this earth is a representation or shadow of what exists in heaven or in the spiritual realm. The family is no exception. For example, concerning marriage we read this in Ephesians 5:31-32, *"For this reason a man shall leave his father and mother and be joined to his wife, and the two shall become one flesh. This is a great mystery, but I speak concerning Christ and the church."* The relationship of

Whether you know it or not, your words, actions, and deeds are painting an image on your child's heart every day. It's an image of God and who they are in relation to Him.

a husband and a wife is very much like, and a physical representation of, the relationship between Christ and the Church. Exchanging the words "husband" and "wife" with "Christ" and the "Church" in the Bible brings a whole new understanding of marriage and the relationship of Jesus to the body of Christ.

Similarly, the development of our children can be viewed as a microcosm of a bigger picture as well: God's plan for the reconciliation of mankind to Himself. In that big picture, we find the road map that will help us guide our children. Read these next few paragraphs carefully. They will lay the foundation for understanding this philosophy.

From the beginning, God has had a plan in place for humankind. When Adam and Eve were created and placed in the Garden of Eden, it was in an age of innocence. They were totally God-conscious, without sin and free of any guilt or condemnation. Only one law existed—they were not to eat of the tree of the knowledge of good and evil. Genesis 2:17 says, *"But of the tree of the knowledge of good and evil you shall not eat, for in the day that you eat of it you shall surely die."*

When they yielded to temptation, sin entered the world and immediately Adam and Eve became self-conscious and sin-conscious. We know that because they were ashamed. Genesis 3:7-8 says this:

Then the eyes of both of them were opened, and they knew that they were naked; and they sewed fig leaves together and made themselves coverings. And they heard the sound of the LORD God walking in the garden in the cool of the day, and Adam and his wife hid themselves from the presence of the LORD God among the trees of the garden.

Shortly after this occurred we see the first prophetic words in the Bible about Jesus. God promised that from woman would come the One who would defeat the enemy and reconcile mankind to God. Genesis 3:15 says, *"And I will put enmity between you and the woman, And between your seed and her Seed; He shall bruise your head, And you shall bruise His heel."* This scripture is specifically talking about the suffering of Jesus and his defeat of the enemy.

Innocence was now lost and the door was opened to a lawless world. People became so depraved that

God was sorry He had made them (Genesis 6:5-7). Except for those on the Ark, all life was destroyed in the flood and would begin anew through the family of Noah.

After the flood, the cycle of human behavior repeated itself again and again. It went from obedience and blessing to apathy, then from apathy to rebellion, and from rebellion to destruction or captivity. Each time God's people repented and cried out for mercy, God faithfully delivered them.

After 400 years of slavery and captivity in Egypt, God raised up Moses to deliver His people. It was through Moses that God delivered and established the Law that the Jewish people still live by today. It spelled out a standard of behavior that God expected them to obey. Human behavior among the Hebrew children would from that time on be governed by a very strict set of laws that carried with them severe consequences if disobeyed. They tried to live by that law, but like all of us, were unsuccessful. Their only consolation, while they waited for the coming of their promised savior, was the offering of sacrifices to cover their sins and clear their consciences.

Then the most important set of events in all of history took place: the birth, death and resurrection of our Savior, Jesus Christ. He became the sacrifice that once and for all reconciled mankind to God. The price for sin was paid in full and our sins are no longer held against us. We entered the age of grace, and by that grace through faith we can be born again and boldly enter into the presence of God without judgment or condemnation.

This was the mystery of all ages that the prophets of old had spoken about. Colossians 1:26-27 says, *"The mystery which has been hidden from ages and from generations, but now has been revealed to His saints. To them God willed to make known what are the riches of the glory of this mystery among the Gentiles: which is Christ in you, the hope of glory."*

Because of what Jesus did, we have a new covenant. As Hebrews 10:16-17 says, *"This is the covenant that I will make with them after those days, says the LORD: I will put My laws into their hearts, and in their minds I will write them, then He adds, Their sins and their lawless deeds I will remember no more."*

This very brief look at biblical history and these tremendous scriptures apply to the family and raising children in a way you may not have considered. They are the core of the philosophy covered in the next several pages. Take time to read the book of Hebrews several times, it will set you free from the Law and help you understand where you need to lead your children.

Reading the Map

There is an incorrect belief or way of thinking that has been accepted as truth in our culture. The Bible calls these ways of thinking "strongholds." (2 Corinthians 10:4,5.) It explains why many liberal thinking people have adopted an approach to raising children that is diametrically opposed to that of a Christian. It's the belief that all human beings are inherently good; that they are born innocent with a human nature yet to be molded. They reject any concept of an inborn sin nature. With that as the premise, they must then conclude that environment determines behavior. Those who believe this deception are convinced that if they can control the environment of their children, which today is nearly impossible, their children will "naturally" do what is right and grow to become good and decent human beings.

A Change of Heart

For those who accept the Word of God as Truth, the very first chapter in the first book of the Bible disproves that theory. Who could ever have a more perfect environment than what Adam and Eve experienced in the garden? They didn't have financial or health problems, abusive parents, drugs or MTV to pollute their mind, or even a heartless employer. God had completely supplied all their human needs. They walked and talked directly with God, and yet they still sinned.

Even if a person doesn't believe the story of Adam and Eve, they have to completely disregard the obvious when a two-year-old throws a fit at the mall because Mom wants to leave the toy store. Was that a learned behavior, or a manifestation of what comes naturally? It should be obvious to any clear thinking person that no one has to teach a child to be selfish and self-centered. It comes naturally because that is the nature of inborn sin.

Jeremiah 17:9 says, *"The heart is deceitful above all things, And desperately wicked; Who can know it?"* In the Greek, the word *deceitful* also means fraudulent, crooked, or polluted and *wicked* means frail, feeble, incurable, and sick. That pretty much describes the condition of the "unrenewed" human heart.

When our children are born, all of us think of them as sweet innocent babies. We as Christians know that, at some point, their true nature will emerge but at least for a while we enjoy that innocence. Predictably, within a short time, our babies become very self-aware or self-conscious just as Adam and Eve did after they sinned. They begin demonstrating selfishness and self-will in a number of ways, forcing the parents to come face to face with the realization that their innocent little baby needs to have its behavior corrected.

What should the parents do? If they're not trying to follow some misguided humanistic approach to raising children, they do exactly what God did through Moses. They establish a set of rules which reward obedience and punish disobedience. They "lay down the law" so to speak.

The Law

The Law was given to the Hebrew people through Moses for three purposes. All three were fulfilled when Jesus rose from the dead and humankind entered the age of grace. And although we are now living under grace, where our young children are concerned, we must still apply the spirit of the Law with those three purposes in mind.

The first purpose was to establish a standard of behavior. Through the Law, God's people were protected and blessed and the society functioned with decency and order. In our family, rules are used to protect our children and bring a sense of order and peace to our home. We use rules to

> *You can't reason with a two year old about the substitutionary sacrifice of Jesus or tell him to walk in the Spirit so he won't fulfill the lust of his flesh (Galatians 5:16).*

train them in proper behavior and help them develop habits that will serve them well as they grow older. Rules are a very necessary part of life while our children are young because they are not yet able to understand spiritual principles.

You can't reason with a two year old about the substitutionary sacrifice of Jesus or tell him to walk in the Spirit so he won't fulfill the lust of his flesh (Galatians 5:16). They can't comprehend that, but what they do understand is that their parents are bigger than they are and that big people have all the power. They very quickly get the concept of reward and consequence and it absolutely affects behavior.

In Galatians 3:23-25 it says, *"But before faith came, we were kept under guard by the law, kept for the faith which would afterward be revealed. Therefore the law was our tutor to bring us to Christ, that we might be*

Have you ever noticed that when you tell your children they can't do something, it's the first thing they want to do?

---

justified by faith. But after faith has come, we are no longer under a tutor." And in Galatians 4:1-2: *"Now I say that the heir, as long as he is a child, does not differ at all from a slave, though he is master of all, but is under guardians and stewards until the time appointed by the father."* The law is like a guardian or a teacher. We use it to teach our children right from wrong and to train them in exercising self-discipline and self-control. Then, when we believe they are ready, we lead them into grace by faith.

The second purpose of the Law was to prove that none of us could keep it. We read that in Romans 3:19-20: *"Now we know that whatever the law says, it says to those who are under the law, that every mouth may be stopped, and all the world may become guilty before God. Therefore by the deeds of the law no flesh will be justified in His sight, for by the law is the knowledge of sin."* Not a single one of us is able to keep the law. If you think you can, then you haven't read James 2:10 which says, *"For whosoever shall keep the whole law, and yet stumble in one point, he is guilty of all."* Combine that with James 4:17: *"Therefore, to him who knows to do good and does not do it, to him it is sin."* Everyone on earth has committed that sin. This should leave little doubt about our inability to meet the standard that God gave to the world through the Law. And if we can't keep God's Law, how can we expect our children to keep our laws or rules?

Have you ever noticed that when you tell your children they can't do something, it's the first thing they want to do? That's because the law actually strengthens sin. 1 Corinthians 15:56 states, *"The sting of death is sin, and the strength of sin is the law."* I recently told one of our grandchildren not to play in the window well of the basement. Five minutes later there he was, building a fort. If I had said nothing, the idea would probably never have occurred to him. That is the way the law works; it strengthens the desire to sin but it also demonstrates our inability to keep it. That failure, which is made apparent through the law, is meant to point us and our children to Jesus Christ and our need for His forgiveness.

The first two purposes of the Law were to control behavior and point us to the need for a savior. The third is at least as important if not more so. While under the law in the home, our children learned to listen and obey because there was not only a threat, but the execution of consequences. As they mature, if we have been effectively shaping their hearts during those times of correction, they will have learned to respond to our words alone. Their willing response becomes practice for them in obeying the voice of the Lord when He speaks to their hearts by the Holy Spirit or through His written Word. In the same way that God places His faith in our willingness to obey His Word, we must eventually place faith in our children's willingness to obey our words. It is in part the evidence of their transition from law to grace.

Once our children are out from under the law and free of the external forces that once held their behavior in check, it is His Word that has been implanted in their hearts and their willingness to listen to His still small voice that will govern their behavior.

Hebrews 10:16-17 says, *"I will put My laws into their hearts, and in their minds I will write them, then*

He adds, Their sins and their lawless deeds I will remember no more." From this scripture and others you have read, it's easy to see that the Lord no longer holds our sins against us. Amazingly, the finished work of grace through Jesus was so complete that God does not even remember our lawless deeds. There is no longer any punishment administered by God for any sin except the sin of rejecting His Son, Jesus. He is the One who became sin for us and received the entire wrath of God's punishment in His flesh. We are redeemed from sin, once for all. (Ephesians 2:15, Colossians 1:20-22; 2:14, Hebrews 10:1-14.)

Following the Lord is strictly voluntary. God has placed His faith in the fact that we will respond to His love and His Word. He does not manipulate or threaten us through the fear of punishment. We are living under a new covenant of grace. God, in His plan, never intended for us to remain under the Law and we cannot keep our children there either.

Galatians 4:4-7 says,

But when the fullness of the time had come, God sent forth His Son, born of a woman, born under the law, to redeem those who were under the law, that we might receive the adoption as sons. And because you are sons, God has sent forth the Spirit of His Son into your hearts, crying out, "Abba, Father!" Therefore you are no longer a slave but a son, and if a son, then an heir of God through Christ.

We must transition our children from living under the bondage of the law to the freedom that is only found in grace as joint heirs with Jesus. Their response to God cannot be the result of external forces or fear; it must come from the heart. The Bible says in Romans 2:4 that it's the goodness of God that leads men to repentance, not judgment and wrath as so many have taught. Our children will best understand this when they see the goodness of God and the love of God for them through us.

In summary, we watch as our children become self-conscious and begin to exhibit self-will. We then establish the rules for their behavior. This sets the stage for a collision between self-will and the law. They may submit or they may rebel, but in either case they become sin-conscious. We spend the early years of their life administering the law to train behavior and establish good habits. Then, the rest of the time we help them transition from law to grace leaving sin-consciousness behind and moving toward the understanding that they are the righteousness of God in Christ Jesus.

It may seem like a contradiction to place your children under the law, then deliver them from it, but it's critical. Unfortunately, many children miss this transition from law to grace and take sin-consciousness with them into adulthood. They continue to live life with the sense that God's blessings and rewards are completely dependent upon their performance.

When the image imprinted on the heart of a child includes guilt, condemnation and sin-consciousness, the result is an adult who finds it very difficult to receive anything from God. They just don't believe they deserve it. Well, guess what? We don't deserve it any more than our children deserve the blessings

We must transition our children from living under the bondage of the law to the freedom that is only found in grace as joint heirs with Jesus.

we bestow on them. They are blessed just because you, their parent, love them. Make sure you don't stop at the law with your children. Lead them a little further to the Grace of God.

I realize that some of the statements I have made may open the door to theological questions that will not be addressed in this book. I recommend two other books written by an excellent Bible teacher, Andrew Wommack. They are *The War is Over* and *Spirit, Soul and Body*. In his books, many questions are answered and you will receive a greater revelation of God's unconditional love and grace. You can find his books and other materials at: **www.awmi.net**.

In the story about Mikey, we see that he had reached an understanding of grace in his life. When Ron knew he was ready, he led him in a prayer to receive Jesus as his Savior. (Read a similar prayer in the back of this book.) From that time on, Mikey's perception and understanding of spiritual things began to grow. 1 Corinthians 2:14 says, *"But the natural man does not receive the things of the Spirit of God, for they are foolishness to him; nor can he know them, because they are spiritually discerned."* Mikey knew he wasn't always obeying Mom and Dad's rules and that he needed the forgiveness of Jesus. The transition from living under the law to walking in the grace of God was beginning to be real to him. From this point forward, Mikey's parents would deal with rebellion in a completely different way.

A Change of Heart

In the next chapter, "A Cage or a Refuge," you will read a story about how a father dealt with rebellion in a teenager. The methodology changed but the goal remained the same - a changed heart.

Discussions Questions
Chapter 3
A Change of Heart

1. Through your words, deeds, and actions, what image of God do you feel you have painted on the canvas of your child's heart?

2. How were you disciplined as a child? Was it from a place of love, or overreaction and anger? From law or grace?

3. How do you think children develop a performance mentality? How might that mentality affect their adult life?

4. How do you think your children see their relationship with you? Does your child see your love as being unconditional, or do you express acceptance and disapproval mostly in connection with how well rules are followed?

5. What strongholds (or incorrect ways of thinking) have you discovered in your own belief system about parenting that need to be torn down?

6. What are some ways you can help your child make the transition from law to grace?

Chapter 4

A Cage or a Refuge?

Gary gradually slowed to a complete stop behind an old diesel pickup. The fumes of dirty exhaust were so strong they were beginning to make him feel nauseous. Looking ahead a mile or so where the interstate curved to the left he could see an ocean of brake lights neatly aligned in six lanes and not one appeared to be moving. What was usually a twenty minute drive home had turned into a bumper to bumper test of endurance and patience.

The temperature gauge on the dash registered 82 degrees on the inside of the car and a sweltering 105 outside. The air conditioner in his ten year old car worked fine at highway speeds but seemed almost useless when sitting in traffic. *Why didn't I add the freon when that mechanic suggested it?* he thought.

Doesn't sound nearly so expensive right now. He leaned forward to turn the fan to high and the mode selector to re-circulate. That gave him the best chance to drop the temperature and eliminate the diesel smell. He felt the welcome relief of a little air moving between the vinyl seat and his sweaty back, but even that didn't help for long.

He reached down and pulled the cell phone from the clip on his belt, flipped open the cover and pressed number one, the speed dial for home. After what seemed to Gary like a hundred rings, Beth finally answered. "Hello?"

"Hi, it's me and I'm stuck in the I-50 parking lot again." She had heard that frustrated tone before and knew he was not going to be in the best of moods when he got home.

"Oh, well. There is nothing you can do about it so just turn on some good music and relax. It will be fine."

"Easy for you to say. It's almost 85 degrees in this car with its sad excuse for an air conditioner," as though he was blaming her for the problem.

"OK. See ya when you get here, bye." She obviously wanted to end the conversation quickly, sensing what might be coming next, the real reason for his call.

"Wait—before you go, did Chris get the yard mowed?"

"No, but it's been a little hot for yard work, don't you think?" Beth was the peacemaker in the family who always looked for a way to defuse tensions, especially when it came to the contentions that always arose between Gary and Chris about yard work.

"What is it about 'mow the yard,' that he doesn't understand? I have told him for the last three days to get the job done. I can guarantee one thing: it will get done today one way or another. Is he there now? I want to talk to him," he insisted.

"He's at Peter's house but he'll be home soon."

"When he gets home, tell him I said not to go anywhere. He and I are going to have a talk about responsibility when I get there."

"Gary, you do need to cool off. You're a little hot all right, but it has nothing to do with the temperature."

Beth loved and respected Gary, but she knew when and how to step in to bring a little perspective to the situation. "We can talk about this when you get here, but right now I have a cake that's ready to come out of the oven."

"OK, but he is still mowing the yard today!"

Thirty minutes later he turned off Walnut Avenue into the driveway. He stopped for a moment to make an assessment of the yard. The grass had grown so tall that it was actually beginning to lay over on itself, making it much more difficult to get an even cut. It was also obvious that it hadn't been edged for at least a couple of weeks. He had always kept the yard perfect and expected Chris to do the same. They had agreed—it was now his responsibility.

Gary pushed the button above the visor for the garage door. As it was opening he could see Chris's old Pontiac Fiero parked on the left side and the lawn mower still sitting against the wall in the corner, undisturbed. He pulled in and released the seat belt with one hand while putting the car in park with the other. The eight steps from the car to the back door in the garage which opened into the family room took about three seconds.

A Cage or a Refuge

He walked in to find Chris sitting comfortably on the couch, feet propped up on the foot stool, watching the Lakers play the Sacramento Kings. "Hi, Pop," he said, as though he had no clue what was on his dad's mind. Chris was a confident sixteen-year-old man. He was responsible, a good student, and generally a great blessing to his parents. There was just something about the yard work that had become a point of contention between father and son. When the subject came up, Beth said it was like watching two bull elk going head-to-head.

Gary expected Chris to respond to him by doing what he asked, when he asked. Chris, on the other hand, felt that since he had been given the responsibility, it was up to him to determine how and when he would carry it out. Chris had conveniently forgotten their discussion and agreements about the how and when of the yard work: once a week, every week, with excellence.

"Don't 'Hi Pop' me, get out there and mow the yard, now!"

"Fine." Chris pushed the footstool away with enough force to send it sliding to the middle of the room and then stood up and walked out, slamming the door to the garage as he left.

Gary wasn't about to leave that unanswered. He immediately jerked the door open and shouted, "You better do a good job, and when you're done, we're going to have a talk."

"Great, I can hardly wait," said Chris.

Gary then closed the door nearly as firmly as Chris had done.

"Well, you sure handled that gracefully," Beth said.

"You know I've been telling him to get this done for days. There's no excuse."

"You might be right, but your attitude stinks just as bad as his, if not worse."

Surprised by her unsympathetic comment, Gary stood there for a moment staring. "I guess I'll go change clothes," he finally said, and then walked down the hall to the bedroom. He sat on the edge of the bed to remove his shoes, then stopped and slowly leaned back, resting his head on the pillow. Beth's words had hit their mark. *She's right,* he thought to himself. *My attitude does stink. What kind of an example was that?*

As he lay there reflecting on the events of the last few minutes, he could hear the drone of the lawn mower coming from the backyard. It usually took Chris about an hour and half to mow and edge, so Gary decided to use that time to get his heart right before confronting Chris. His attitude had certainly provoked Chris, and he knew it. *Chris was now complying; he was getting the work done, and it would sure be a lot easier to let it end here,* he thought to himself. But Gary knew he still had to fulfill his responsibility and confront the rebellion Chris had demonstrated. And he needed to address the more important underlying problem, the issue of the heart.

The Lord began speaking to Gary, reminding him of scriptures like Ephesians 6:12, *"For we do not wrestle against flesh and blood, but against principalities, against powers, against the rulers of the darkness of this age, against spiritual hosts of wickedness in the heavenly places."* And Ephesians 6:4, *"And you, fathers, do not provoke your children to wrath, but bring them up in the training and admonition of the Lord".* He had just violated the message of both of those scriptures.

In the past, the devil could have used those same scriptures to judge and condemn Gary. But over the years he had finally come to understand that it wasn't the Lord who condemns and accuses. That was the work of the enemy. The Lord, by His love, was using His Word to correct, to soften Gary's heart and change his attitude. He began thinking about how much God loved him and Chris, and that His desire was to bring reconciliation and peace. The Word was beginning to have its effect on Gary, as it says in Hebrew 4:12: *"For the word of God is living and powerful, and sharper than any two-edged sword, piercing even to the division of soul and spirit, and of joints and marrow, and is a discerner of the thoughts and intents of the heart."* It wasn't condemnation and judgment that Gary was feeling from the Lord; it was love, acceptance and forgiveness. This was not the way he had just dealt with his son.

The lawn mower was now silent and within a few minutes he heard Chris coming down the hall headed for the shower. "Hey, Chris?"

"Yeah."

"After you get cleaned up, I want to talk with you, OK?"

"Sure, I'm up for a lecture."

By now, Gary's heart and attitude had changed although it was obvious by that smart remark that Chris's had not. What would have angered Gary an hour earlier now only served to increase his desire to bring about reconciliation. Now, it was his love for Chris that motivated him, not anger, not a need to prove his point or to assert his authority as the head of the home.

He understood his position and accepted the responsibility that came with it. He knew that it was a type and shadow of the position Jesus has as the head of the Church; He leads by example and by serving, not force. Submission to Him is voluntary under the grace in which we now live and Chris's submission to Gary needed to be voluntary as well. Chris had

> *Now, it was his love for Chris that motivated him, not anger, not a need to prove his point or to assert his authority as the head of the home.*

long since transitioned from being under the law as a little boy to walking in grace as a young man. It would have to be the love of God and the love of a father that would draw him and the power of the Word of God that would change his heart.

Gary was now in the right frame of mind to be a vessel for the Lord to bring about reconciliation and contend for the heart of his son. He gave Chris time to dress and then knocked on the door.

"Can I come in for a few minutes?"

"Sure." Chris was sitting on the bed so Gary pulled up the desk chair and positioned it where he could face him.

"Chris, I love you and I'm sorry. I wasn't in a good mood on the way home and when I learned that the yard had not yet been mowed after asking you several times, well, I reacted in anger. I have been in my room praying, getting my heart right and my attitude changed. Will you forgive me for my bad attitude and raising my voice the way I did?"

"Sure, Dad."

"Thanks, we both know I don't always get it right." The "sure Dad" wasn't all that sincere but Gary's apology was. True humility was a big part of what gave Gary the right to be heard.

Hebrews 4:15 and 5:8-9 say, *"For we do not have a High Priest who cannot sympathize with our weaknesses, but was in all points tempted as we are, yet without sin. Though He was a Son, yet He learned obedience by the things which He suffered. And having been perfected, He became the author of eternal salvation to all who obey Him."*

Even though Jesus was God in the flesh, He had to earn the right to lead and be heard. God understood how important it was for us to see the humanity of Jesus, even though unlike us, He was without sin. He was born in obscurity and lived a simple life as the son of a carpenter until the beginning of His ministry. He endured temptation as we all do, and learned obedience to the Father through the things that he suffered.

When the disciples James and John asked to sit beside Him in Glory, His reply exemplified His character and nature. Mark 10:44-45 says, *"And whoever of you desires to be first shall be slave of all. For even the Son of Man did not come to be served, but to serve, and to give His life a ransom for many."* As parents, we should learn from His words and example. Our children need to see us for who we are: imperfect human beings, willing to humble ourselves and lay down our lives (the cares of the world, the lusts of the flesh and deceitfulness of riches) for their sake.

"We're not finished yet." Gary said.

"Yeah, I figured that," Chris said with a sigh.

"Chris, as I look into your eyes I can see the anger and resentment. It's like looking into the window of your soul and there is no way to hide what's in your heart."

Contending for the Heart

Gary knew it wasn't Chris that he was fighting now. He was dealing with the *spirit of rebellion*. It was contending for the heart of his son and he was not about to let it win. He was armed with the knowledge that the One living in him was greater than the one in the world (1 John 4:4).

"Chris, you have heard me say this before, but I am saying it again. You are a terrific young man. You're a man of God and you have a destiny that God planned just for you. However, it is up to you whether or not it's fulfilled. The only one that can ever stop that destiny from coming to pass is you. We have talked about rebellion and the effect it can have in your life many times and that I have the responsibility to help you overcome in this area. I want to read a little from Hebrews 12:7-8,&11:

'If you endure chastening, God deals with you as with sons; for what son is there whom a father does not chasten? But if you are without chastening, of which all have become partakers, then you are illegitimate and not sons. Furthermore, we have had human fathers who corrected us, and we paid them

respect. Shall we not much more readily be in subjection to the Father of spirits and live? Now no chastening seems to be joyful for the present, but painful; nevertheless, afterward it yields the peaceable fruit of righteousness to those who have been trained by it.'

"What we are doing now is not comfortable for either of us, but we are going to stay here until God has changed our hearts toward each other and toward Him." Chris just sat there, staring at the wall, seemingly unmoved by his Dad's oration.

"I think about the children of Israel," Gary continued, "who were never allowed by God to enter into the promise land because of disobedience. The Bible says that their hearts always went astray. It led to an evil heart of unbelief which destroyed their faith. Without faith they were unable to see themselves overcoming the giants in the land and fulfilling their destiny. It will take faith for you to fulfill your destiny as well, and I won't allow rebellion to steal that from you. This is too important to ignore, I can't let this slide today or any other day. I love you too much for that."

Gary continued on, mixing his words with the Word of God, never using them like a hammer to pound Chris into submission with blows of judgment and condemnation. He used them like a healing ointment, to soften the heart of stone and turn it once again into a pliable heart of clay.

Chris seemed almost unmoved, saying nothing, but Gary noticed that his body language was beginning to change. He was now leaning forward with his arms resting on his thighs and hands folded. His head was bowed as he stared at the floor. The resistance that had almost been palpable was subsiding.

Gary continued on, mixing his words with the Words of God, never using them like a hammer to pound Chris into submission with blows of judgment and condemnation.

The Holy Spirit, through the words that were spoken, was changing the atmosphere and the heart.

Gary perceived what was happening and slowly stood to his feet, "Chris, stand up with me for a minute, would you please?" Chris and Gary were both six feet tall and they were now toe to toe looking at each other square in the eyes about 18 inches apart. Gary placed one hand on each of Chris's shoulders. Pulling him forward he whispered these words in his ear: "I love you son, I love you."

The compassion of his words could not be resisted. Chris slowly lowered his head and rested it on his dad's shoulder and then put his arms around him, gradually tightening his hug. Gary could now hear him beginning to weep softly.

Then Chris whispered, "I love you too Dad. I'm sorry for the way I acted." They stood unashamedly with tears running down their cheeks, holding each other for several minutes. Then, almost as if on cue, they both sat down and smiled as they wiped away the tears.

2 Corinthians 5:18-20 says,

Now all things are of God, who has reconciled us to Himself through Jesus Christ, and has given us the ministry of reconciliation, that is, that God was in Christ reconciling the world to Himself, not imputing their trespasses to them, and has committed to us the word of reconciliation. Now then, we are ambassadors for Christ, as though God were pleading through us: we implore you on Christ's behalf, be reconciled to God.

Gary had acted as an ambassador of Christ. God was pleading through him to bring reconciliation first between Chris and God and second between Chris and his dad. Nearly an hour had passed from the time Gary entered Chris's room until that moment of reconciliation. There are no shortcuts when you're expecting more than mere compliance and submission. Those can be obtained by simply applying enough external pressure, like Gary had wrongly done when he first came home. It took time for the Holy Spirit to work in Chris's heart and for him to respond. Gary had nearly fallen back into the trap of doing the expedient; using the law to overcome rebellion and force a change in behavior instead of trusting the Lord to work in the heart.

There are no shortcuts when you're expecting more than mere compliance and submission.

That is exactly how a home can become a cage instead of a refuge. We can't ignore rebellion; it must be confronted. If it is not, the heart becomes more calloused and the manifestations of the rebellion progressively become worse. If it isn't dealt with at the heart level, then the measures that must be taken to restrict or control the behaviors will force you to turn your home into a cage.

A Cage or a Refuge

Reconciliation might look like the end to this story, but it was really just the beginning. The rebellious spirit which was contending for the heart of Chris had lost the battle again. But the emotions and vulnerabilities that surfaced in this rich time created an open door of opportunity.

Over the next hour, Gary and Chris sat man to man as friends, discussing issues of life, iron sharpening iron. Proverbs 27:17 states, *"As iron sharpens iron; so a man sharpens the countenance of his friend."* The superglue of love and respect was binding their hearts together in a way that no human being or devil could ever tear apart.

———⚬∘⚬———

"Chris, we are born again in our spirit, but still living in a human body. In our own strength and power none of us are able to live the life we desire in our heart."

———⚬∘⚬———

At one point, Chris asked his father a very revealing question, one that all of us ask at some time or another: "Why do I act this way Dad? I really don't want to, but I do it anyway. What's wrong with me?"

The answer went something like this: "Chris, we are born again in our spirit, but still living in a human body. In our own strength and power none of us are able to live the life we desire in our heart." The Apostle Paul said this in Roman 7:18-21:

For I know that in me (that is, in my flesh) nothing good dwells; for to will is present with me, but how to perform what is good I do not find. For the good that I will to do, I do not do; but the evil I will not to do, that I practice. Now if I do what I will not to do, it is no longer I who do it, but sin that dwells in me. I find then a law, that evil is present with me, the one who wills to do good.

Gary went on to say, "But Paul does not leave us with a sense of hopelessness. He goes on to give us great hope in the power of His grace to set us free from this dilemma. This marvelous act of grace on God's part through Jesus Christ has set us free from sin and death." Romans 8:1-4 says,

"The answer to walking in the Spirit does not lie in self-control or self-discipline, Chris; these will fail you sooner or later."

There is therefore now no condemnation to those who are in Christ Jesus, who do not walk according to the flesh, but according to the Spirit. For the law of the Spirit of life in Christ Jesus has made me free from the law of sin and death. For what the law could not do in that it was weak through the flesh, God did by sending His own Son in the likeness of sinful flesh, on account of sin: He condemned sin in the flesh, that the righteous requirement of the law might be fulfilled in us who do not walk according to the flesh but according to the Spirit.

"The answer to walking in the Spirit does not lie in self-control or self-discipline, Chris; these will fail you sooner or later. We both experienced that today in our own actions. The secret is to depend on Him and to allow Him to change our hearts and adjust our attitudes. If we will do that, the right behavior will always follow."

Both Gary and Chris grew a little that day. Their relationship was again strengthened through a confrontation that was carefully directed toward a changed heart, reconciliation, and building foundations through heartfelt communication.

Years later, after Chris was married and the father of two, he and Gary met at a coffee shop. They were talking about a whole lot of nothing when suddenly Chris said, "Dad, I just wanted to thank you for teaching me how to say I'm sorry and how to bring about reconciliation in my family. It has brought so much peace to our home. I just wanted you to know that." It was all Gary could do to keep from crying in front of the thirty or so strangers at the cafe. What greater reward could a father have than to hear those words from his son?

Galatians 6:9 says, *"And let us not grow weary while doing good, for in due season we shall reap if we do not lose heart."* Gary was reaping the priceless reward of the years of diligent effort and sacrifice.

When our children are very young, it is necessary to control their behavior by using the law, enforced with certain consequence, to set the standard and point them to their need for a Savior. The law also helps us teach them to listen to our words. In the story of Gary and Chris, if Chris had not been willing to listen, the heart may never have been changed.

A Cage or a Refuge

Hebrews 5:13-14 says, *"For everyone who partakes only of milk is unskilled in the word of righteousness, for he is a babe. But solid food belongs to those who are of full age, that is, those who by reason of use have their senses exercised, to discern both good and evil."* By constant reinforcement, or reason of use, as a boy, Chris had developed the habit of listening, trusting,

> Gary and Beth both understood that parenting is really the art of becoming not needed.

and responding to his parent's words. They had moved from the milk of the Word, which in this example is the law, to the meat of the Word, which is operating in the power of God's grace. Working with your children in grace takes more thought and effort; but if you will look ahead, you will see that it is well worth it.

Gary and Beth both understood that parenting is really the art of becoming not needed. Many parents misunderstand that. They think it means training their children to become self-sufficient, self-disciplined and self-confident. Attempting to maintain those character traits without deep roots in the Lord is impossible for any human being. What parents should be doing is transferring their children's dependence upon them to a dependence upon God. Their confidence and sufficiency should be in Him and no longer in their parents. Self-discipline and self-control flow from a relationship with the Lord, not from human effort.

If our children understand this, they will be able to live their life as independent thinkers because they trust the One who orders their footsteps. Psalms 119:133 says, *"Direct my steps by Your word, And let no iniquity have dominion over me."* The fruit of pursuing a destiny ordered and directed by God will be restraint, self-discipline, self-control, and confidence in who they are in Him.

Gary and Beth also understood that their son was no longer a boy, but a man. They had not allowed themselves to be misguided by the myth of adolescence. If you believe adolescence is a reality that all parents must face, then read the next chapter.

Discussions Questions
Chapter 4
A Cage or a Refuge

1. What spirits or opposing forces are contending for your child's heart, and for the heart of your family?

2. What scriptures has the devil twisted and used to bring you under condemnation?

3. In what ways do you think it is important to lead by example? Are there areas of your life that you feel you could become a better role model?

4. How should you confront rebellion in your child?

5. What do you think the effect on your child's behavior will be if he or she perceives your home as a cage?

6. What might the effect on your child be if he or she feels that your home is a refuge and a sanctuary from the world? What can you do to make your home a refuge?

Chapter 5

The Myth of Adolescence

Saturday morning turned out to be exceptional. The clear blue sky and mild temperature had combined to make it a perfect day for a track meet. Bill always enjoyed sitting in the bleachers with the other parents and members of the team. There was plenty of time between events to hear the latest news from friends about family and work while sparring a little with the athletes. They all loved to tease and seemed to enjoy interacting with the parents.

It was nearly time for the 800 meter, Bill's favorite race and one that Jason had a very good chance of winning. Five schools were represented and the competition looked strong. This two lap race was not purely a sprint nor an endurance race, but a little of both and that's what really made it tough. Although physical strength was very important, the one with the most heart usually won. Bill stood up to get a better look at Jason's competitors as they moved to their starting positions. *I wonder if he can beat that senior from Woodman Academy?* he thought.

He felt the sweat trickling from under his arms and slowly running down his sides as his heart began to beat faster and faster. Lifting the binoculars to get a closer look he realized they were smeared so badly he could hardly see. "Anyone got a Kleenex?" he hollered impatiently, hoping someone could help.

"Here ya go Bill, this should work," said one of the moms as she handed him a napkin from a backpack.

"Thanks." He quickly cleaned the lens, not wanting to miss a thing. *OK, take a breath and relax, he'll do fine,* he thought to himself.

Jason, on the other hand, seemed perfectly calm, smiling at the crowd as he walked slowly to the starting blocks, stopping to stretch along the way. The runners politely acknowledged each other and then took their places for the staggered start. A few of the stronger competitors recognized Jason from previous meets and from the look on their faces they seemed to know that he would be someone to contend with down the stretch.

The Myth of Adolescence

The command came: "On your mark....set...." and at the sound of the starting gun, the runners exploded out of the blocks to position themselves for the move back to the inside lane.

Jason had learned to pace himself and stay in the middle of the pack but always within reach of the leader. Bill watched intently as the first lap was predictably completed with the runners tightly bunched. That was really considered the warm up. It was the second lap where the race began in earnest and the strategies would play out. They rounded the first turn of the second lap and he could see Jason gradually quickening his pace and moving forward. The three leaders, which included Jason, separated themselves from the pack on the back stretch and entered the third corner with about 150 meters to go.

Jason was running shoulder to shoulder with the leader when the guy suddenly moved to the right causing Jason to stumble. Bill couldn't believe his eyes. "Oh no," he gasped. Through the binoculars it was obvious to him that the bump had been intentional. Jason had managed to stay on his feet but was now at least three meters behind. For a second, it looked like the race was over, but then he got a glimpse of Jason's face.

Instead of resignation, there was a look of anger and determination; he wasn't about to give up and Bill knew it. Reaching deep into his reservoir of courage, Jason went into high gear and began to close. As they turned for home, the crowd, sensing what was about to happen, stood to their feet to cheer the runners on. Both runners were now grimacing with pain as their muscles began to tighten up from the lactic acid. Without a doubt, this race would go to the one with the most heart.

"Go, go, go," Bill shouted as he dropped the binoculars to get a better look at the finish line. He could hardly contain himself as Jason crossed the line first, just inches ahead. "That's my boy," he said as if it was exactly what he expected to happen.

The crowd roared and Jason's teammates swarmed as he dropped to one knee, completely exhausted. Bill also felt pats on the back as the other parents congratulated him, but he never took his eyes off Jason. He knew that Jason would soon look to the stands for that smile of approval from Dad. It was an unspoken ritual that meant a lot to them both. He wasn't disappointed.

When things quieted, Bill sat down and thought back to an event in Jason's life a few years earlier.

The Myth of Adolescence

Bill and his wife had made a conscious decision to treat Jason like a man and he was living up to those expectations. They had told him for years that when he was thirteen he would be accepted as a man. On his thirteenth birthday they invited his grandparents, his uncles, and a few other respected leaders that had influenced his life to their home. This would become his rite of passage.

After dinner, they all gathered around Jason. Bill laid his hands on his son and led in a prayer. "Jason, I declare tonight that you are a man and will be treated as such by your mother and me from this day forward. I bless you with a father's blessing as Jacob blessed the sons of Joseph." Bill continued with many specifics about the kind of man Jason was and how he believed God was going to use him in the future. Jason's mother followed Bill in much the same fashion and then the others present were given the opportunity to speak into his life as well.

From then on, Jason was included in making family decisions, not in word only, but in deed. His opinion was valued by his father, mother and grandparents. In conducting themselves this way, Jason saw himself as a man with responsibility. They continually reinforced the idea that he had a destiny. Even though they did not know the specifics of that destiny they encouraged him to prepare and set goals in line with his natural gifts and talents. That day had been a turning point in Jason's life that Bill knew was helping guide his son's life.

His thoughts returned to the present when he noticed Jason walking back and forth very slowly. He was obviously in pain massaging that big muscle on his back side as he walked. Concerned, he left his seat and walked to the infield where Jason was standing, obviously in pain. The cramp that followed his extraordinary effort had almost brought him to tears.

"Are you all right?" Bill said after an enthusiastic high five.

"Yeah Dad, but it sure hurts!"

Bill put his arms around Jason's sweaty neck and gave him a big hug. "That was the gutsiest race I have ever seen a man run," he said. "Not very many men have that kind of courage and determination. I'm so proud of you."

"Thanks, Dad."

Jason understood that it wasn't the win that his father was referring to—although that was great. It was the demonstration of character and heart that made his dad so proud. He was hearing again, from the person whose opinion he valued the most, that he had what it took to be a man.

Deep in the heart of every boy there are two important questions waiting to be answered. *What does it take to become a man? and How will I know when I have arrived?* In our culture today, these critical questions about manhood are almost always left unanswered. Most of us men have been forced to figure out the mystery of becoming a man for ourselves. Defining and establishing this in the heart of our sons has been a missing ingredient in our culture for many years. It has left millions of young men anxious to validate their manhood any way they can. When we leave it to the world to make this definition and determine the criteria for that validation, it becomes distorted at best and perverted at worst.

Not only does this apply to our sons, but to our daughters as well. Every young boy wants to know when he will be considered a man and every young girl wants to know when she is considered a woman.

It is up to us as parents to make that clear, and to do this we must know the truth ourselves.

There is absolutely no foundation for the myth of adolescence anywhere in the Bible. It has only been in recent history that this myth has been widely accepted as truth by the majority of people in the Western world. It has become so ingrained in the minds of parents that many dread the day their children become teens.

The psychologist, Granville Stanley Hall, introduced the concept of adolescence to America in the late 19th century. Once on his way to becoming a minister, he shifted gears, and in 1878 earned the first Ph.D. of psychology granted in America from Harvard University. By the middle of the 20th century his ideas and those of other like-minded men had become the norm in higher education. Sadly, many Christian leaders in the church were also accepting these concepts as truth.

Educators, psychologists and other proponents of adolescence have managed to convince the world that teenagers are unable to make good decisions and if not closely supervised would live irresponsible, undisciplined lives. Sigmund Freud

The Myth of Adolescence

wrote this in an essay he published; "Adolescence is a period of emotional upheaval, inconsistent behavior, and vulnerability to deviant and criminal activity caused by psychosexual conflicts." Well, to that I reply, the wisdom of man is but foolishness to God. (1 Corinthians 3:19.) I have never read anything about adolescence in the Bible but I have read much about God's opinion of the human philosophy of this world.

The belief in the myth of adolescence becomes a self-fulfilling prophesy within the family. In essence, we have given our children permission and willingly accepted the fact that they are going to act irresponsibly between the ages of 13 and 21. We are by silent consent, giving them permission to experiment and do what is often referred to as "discover themselves." We are setting them up to waste an entire decade convinced that they are neither children nor adults.

Proverbs 29:18 says in the King James version, *"Where there is no vision, the people perish"* and in the New King James, *"Where there is no revelation, the people cast off restraint."* When we leave our children without vision and purpose, allowing them to "discover themselves", they easily become unrestrained. Their deep desire and need to accomplish something of value is replaced with the pursuit of pleasure and fulfillment of the flesh.

Young men and women have a deep desire to make their life count. Not only do they have this desire but they also have the capability to do so if we will help them prepare. John Quincy Adams, who would one day become president, left his father and traveled to Holland to attend Leyden University at age 14. He was made secretary and French interpreter for Francis Dana, the American Ambassador to Russia. He traveled the continent alone, through numerous European nations, overcoming many language and culture barriers. At 15 he returned from St. Petersburg, Russia, to The Hague which entailed an overland journey of six months. At 16, he was made the secretary to the American commissioners in France negotiating the peace treaty with Great Britain to end the Revolutionary War. At 17, he returned to the United States to begin studies at Harvard, his second university.

Louisa May Alcott, who lived from 1832 to 1888, was an author and teacher. She was writing poetry at the age of eight, with her mother telling her that "if she kept on in this hopeful way, she might be a second Shakespeare in time." Only five years later, when 13, she wrote a famous poem, "My Kingdom". At 16, she wrote a book, *Flower Fables*; at 18, she wrote the novel, *Moods*; and at 19, her stories were being published in magazines across the country.

William Frederick "Buffalo Bill" Cody became a paid cowhand at nine. At 11, he was making long cattle drives and by 12, he had become a trapper and woodsman. At 13, he became a Pony Express rider. At 15, he was riding military dispatches, and at 16 he was a guide and scout for the military. He eventually became a Medal of Honor winner.

James Iredell lived from 1751 to 1799. He was a Government Financial Officer, Justice of the U.S. Supreme Court, and a Ratifier of the U.S. Constitution. At 17, he was the comptroller of the Customs House in Edenton, North Carolina. By the time he was 23, his political writing in favor of America had made him the most influential political writer in North Carolina.

Maria Mitchell, an astronomer and teacher, lived from 1818 to 1889. At 11, she became a teaching assistant while at the same time studying astronomy. At 12, she helped calculate the exact time of a forthcoming total solar eclipse, quite a feat in her time. At 17, she was the head of her own academy.

These are just a few examples of literally thousands of young people who have accomplished great things. As a whole, the myth of adolescence has almost single-handedly destroyed our confidence in the capabilities of young people and lowered our expectations of the youth of our nation. It doesn't have to be that way with your children.

Paul writes in 1 Corinthians 13:11, *"When I was a child, I spoke as a child, I understood as a child, I thought as a child; but when I became a man, I put away childish things."* Paul did not indicate that there was any time gap between childhood and manhood. In the Jewish culture of his day you were still considered a child at 12, but when young boys turned 13 they went through a rite of passage called the bar mitzvah. From that day on, they were accepted into the world of men. For young women the same ritual

> *As a whole, the myth of adolescence has almost single-handedly destroyed our confidence in their capabilities and lowered our expectations of the youth of our nation.*

is called the bat mitzvah. This is just as important an event for our daughters as for our sons.

God in His wisdom uses puberty to mark the demarcation between childhood and the beginning of adulthood. Look at the definition of the word puberty. It comes from the Latin words *pubertas*, which means "the age or condition of physical maturity," and *pubes*, which means "a grown-up person, adult."

The world is constantly sending mixed signals about adulthood. You can drive when you're 16, sign a contract at 18, drink hard liquor at 21, yet be tried as an adult for a violent crime as a young teenager, and if some lawmakers have their way, have an abortion at 13 without parental consent or notification. It is no wonder that so many are confused about this issue.

The best book I have read on this subject is *Men of Honor and Women of Virtue* by Dr. Chuck Stecker. He writes, "One of the primary purposes of the rite of passage into adulthood is to give parents, children, and churches a clear starting line for the journey called 'adulthood and spiritual maturity.' Never has the need for concrete rites of passage into adulthood been as critical in our churches and families as it is today." In his book he defines the difference between adulthood and maturity. The fact that our children are adults does not mean they are mature in every way. Maturity is a process; even Jesus did not step into His ministry until he was thirty. Though He was God in the flesh, He was also human, and had much to learn before He was ready to lead.

This is important to understand because it will determine how you deal with your children as teenagers. Contending for the heart of a teen must be approached differently than a young child. They are adults who should have transitioned from living under the requirements of the law to the freedom of grace.

Once you have accepted your child as an adult it doesn't eliminate the need to correct their behavior, but the methods change with age. As you have read in the previous stories, the goal is always the same, a change in heart.

Discussions Questions
Chapter 5
The Myth of Adolescence

1. What myths about adolescence do you believe? What myths were you told about adolescence while you were growing up?

2. How are you acknowledging your child when he or she demonstrates character?

3. Why do children value the opinions of their parents? What effect do you think your opinion is having on your child?

4. What are some ways you can define, establish, and validate the transition to adulthood in the heart of your son or daughter?

5. Are your children demonstrating levels of maturity? What responsibilities can your child assume at this current age?

Contending for the Heart

Chapter 6

The Power of Influence

Mark was sitting quietly in his favorite armchair with a magazine in hand, but he wasn't reading. Without moving his head, he peered over the rim of his reading glasses at the grandfather clock next to the fireplace. The second hand seemed to stand still. Jan was trying to look busy cleaning up after supper but her thoughts had little to do with the kitchen. Both of them were waiting for their treasured Sunday evening call.

Sarah was completing her education and living on her own for the first time, eleven hundred miles away. She was excited about the future and was adjusting quickly to her new life. Mom and Dad, on the other hand, often found themselves standing at the door of her bedroom across the hall. The bed was undisturbed with the pillows neatly arranged against the headboard. The lamp, pictures, and artificial flowers were all in their place. A few months earlier it would have been difficult to hang one more thing in the closet, but now it stood empty.

Mark's eyes glazed over as he thought back to a special day nearly a year earlier and the events that followed. "I'll be waiting in the car," Mark said impatiently, as he passed by Sarah's room on the way to the garage. As usual, he was ready a little early and she would again manage to be just a little late. He had been anticipating this date with his daughter, Sarah, for the last several days. Their dates were always great, but this one was especially meaningful, as it would be their last for a long time.

Some thought it strange to see a beautiful young woman walking hand-in-hand with a much older man; their disapproving looks revealing the dark thoughts of their hearts. But Mark and Sarah were not at all embarrassed as they strolled along Pier 39 in San Francisco. She had held his hand while walking together for the last 21 years and they saw no reason to change that tradition. Lunch at Bubba Gump's overlooking the bay, a trolley car ride through Chinatown, a stroll down Fisherman's Wharf, and the day was coming to an end much too soon. But they had made a memory, a very special one for both of them.

The following Friday evening, one short week later, they were pulling into the driveway of a good friend in Colorado Springs. They had arranged for Sarah to stay with them for a few days until her apartment was ready. It was very comforting to know that a trusted friend would be there for their daughter if she needed help. Saturday flew by running errands, driving Sarah to a job interview, and helping her get a feel for the city.

Sunday morning was the scheduled departure time and it came much too quickly. Mark, Jan, Sarah and their friends all lingered at the table long after breakfast was finished. *How do you say good-bye to your only daughter who has been your princess for the past twenty one years?* Mark thought. He knew letting go would not be easy but this was going to be even more difficult than he imagined.

He finally stood to his feet, "Well Honey, we have to get on the road." Sarah immediately pushed her chair back from the table, jumped up, and ran out the front door. Mark and Jan said goodbye to their friends, thanking them for all they had done, and then headed out the door to Sarah who was now leaning against the car sobbing. There was little left to say, it was time for hugs and kisses interrupted only by "I love you." The word "goodbye" was never spoken.

Tears streaming down their cheeks, Mark and Jan finally pulled away and headed back to California. The first few hours in the car were spent in silence as they allowed the emotions of the moment to slowly subside. Mark and Jan knew that their daughter's move to Colorado had greater implications than the completion of her education. It was the beginning of a new chapter in her life; one that was difficult for them but filled with hope and expectation for her.

One of those expectations was about to be realized.

The first ring of the phone startled Mark; he had been completely caught up in the emotion of his memories. But by the second ring, he was reaching for the phone.

"Hello."

"It's her," he said. Jan had already picked up the other receiver.

"Hi Mom, Hi Dad."

"Hi Honey, how are you?"

The Power of Influence

"I'm doing great, Dad" she said with the same delight that he used to hear in her voice as a little girl on Christmas morning. It was a playful tone that was really saying, *Guess what?* She had a story to tell but it would have to wait until Jan had heard all the details of how the week had gone. Within a few minutes, the week's events had been thoroughly explored and it was time for Dad to try and guess what she really wanted to talk about.

"So tell us, what's on your mind? Did you meet a man?"

"Well, maybe."

Sarah was a beautiful woman. She had made two important decisions early in life. She wouldn't date until she was serious about marriage, and she would keep herself for her future husband. Her mom and dad had told her from the time she was old enough to understand, that she was a princess and that God would bring her a prince in shining armor. All she needed to do was trust Him and act like a princess. She believed them!

"So, what's his name?"

"Jeff."

Then, purposely exaggerating the words he asked, "Is he tall, dark, and handsome?"

"Well…..I think so," then she proceeded to tell them that she had met him at church. Jeff was a couple of years older than her, well educated, and seemed to have a vision for his life. Besides all of that, he was a leader in the young adult group at church and was renting a room from the pastor. She had learned all this over a lunch and a dinner date.

After listening to the long list of Jeff's credentials, Mark said the obvious, "What's not to like?" And without a moment's hesitation he followed that remark with the really big question. "Do you feel like there could be sparks between you and him?"

There was silence for a moment before her thoughtful reply, "Yes, there could be."

"Well then, you know the next step, right?"

"What step would that be, Dad?"

"You know, have him give me a call next week and I'll talk with him."

"Well, OK Dad, but be nice," she insisted.

"You know I will. Tell him I'll be expecting to hear from him in the next few days."

The Power of Influence

The call ended all too soon, but Mark and Jan continued late into the night, discussing what they had just heard and the implications it might have in Sarah's life.

The next evening Jeff called.

"Hello, Mr. Barnes, I believe you are expecting my call."

"Hi Jeff, I was, and thanks for calling so promptly."

Mark motioned for Jan to pick up the extension.

He continued, "Sarah tells me she has been seeing you and I just wanted to get to know you a little. Would that be all right?"

"Sure, what would you like to know?"

First came the ice breaker questions, like "Where are you from?", "Tell me a little about your family" and "What do you plan to do in the future?" Jeff answered and soon became very comfortable talking with Mark, so much so that he was communicating information about himself that had not been solicited. Mark, on the other hand, was becoming less comfortable. He began to sense something about this young man that didn't quite seem right. He couldn't put his finger on it, but felt that he and Jan needed to know more before a bond developed between the two. What he said next surprised even Jan.

"Jeff , I would like to talk with your parents and also the pastor you're living with, would that be OK?"

"Yes, sir."

"Good, now until you hear from me again, this is what I want you to promise me. I don't want you to have any kind of physical intimacy with Sarah, including holding hands, embracing, hugging, or kissing. Do I have your word on that?"

"Yes, sir, you do."

"Thank you Jeff, it's been nice speaking with you and I hope to talk with you again soon."

After they hung up, Jan looked at Mark in disbelief, "I can't believe you said that to him."

"Me either." Even Mark was surprised at himself.

The next evening the phone rang again. It was Sarah.

"Hello."

"Hi Dad," she said, and without a moment's pause for his response, "What in the world did you say to Jeff?"

"Why, what happened?"

"I just got off the phone with him and any relationship that was developing is over."

"Really? Tell us more." By this time Jan was on the extension listening intently.

"He said that he had talked with you and after thinking about it felt it was only fair that he make me aware of his past before we went any further. He told me he had a girl friend a few years ago and that they had an intimate sexual relationship. He said he knew it was wrong and that he had repented and asked God to forgive him. Then he asked me if I would be able to continue seeing him knowing about this history. And Dad, he told me he loved me."

"So, how did you answer him?"

"I told him I understood and think he is really a great guy, but that is not what I am believing for in my future husband. I tried to be kind, but I told him that our relationship was over." Then she paused, "You and Mom have always told me that I would get a prince, and I believe you!"

"You will, too," they assured her.

The rest of the evening Mark and Jan discussed what had transpired. Their daughter had done exactly what they hoped she would. But her last words were weighing on Mark's heart, "I believe you." Had he made a mistake in placing so much emphasis on promising his daughter that God would bring the right man and that he would not have any baggage? Could this have been the right man? After all, Jeff had acted with real integrity thus far. Perhaps he had turned his life around. Mark struggled with doubts for the next few days.

Mark and Jan had contended for their daughter's heart all her life. Through their words, actions, and deeds they had helped her paint an image of her husband on the canvas of her heart. And when Jeff asked the question, she simply searched her heart for the answer. The image there had become so clear that she was never really in doubt. She would wait for the man who would fulfill that image.

Amazingly, only two weeks later Sarah met another young man whose name was also Jeff. The involvement of her father took a similar path but the result was completely different. After talking with him on several occasions, Mark and Jan both felt like the Lord had brought Sarah her future husband. They didn't tell her that at the time, but after their first face-to-face meeting with Jeff on a trip to Colorado, they let her know she had their blessing.

The Power of Influence

It was months later Mark and Jan learned Jeff's story. Two weeks before meeting Sarah, he had an interesting discussion with his father. He said, "Dad, I'm 25 years old and I feel like I have been waiting a long time for the right girl. I want to get married but I have not been able to find a real princess."

His father encouraged him not to get anxious and make a mistake. "It's better to be single wishing you were married, than married wishing you were single."

Two weeks later he met Sarah, literally the girl of his dreams. Jeff told Mark that he had a dream when he was much younger concerning the woman he would marry and that Sarah was that girl. The first time he saw her he had a sense he had just met his future bride. Six months later they were engaged, and six months following the engagement, they were married.

Would things have worked out with Jeff #1? Maybe, only God knows. But at the time of this writing, Sarah and Jeff #2 are celebrating their 14th anniversary. Their marriage is solid and they now have three wonderful children of their own. Both Sarah and Jeff had the faith and courage to wait for the right person. They both had the encouragement of their parents to reinforce what they believed in their hearts. Their decisions were not by chance or accident; they were simply making decisions according to the boundaries that had been established in their hearts.

Proverbs 4:23 KJV reminds us to *"Keep thy heart with all diligence; for out of it are the issues (boundaries and borders) of life."*

When the angel of the Lord came to King Solomon and asked him what he wanted, Solomon asked for wisdom.

2 Chronicles 1:7-12 says,

On that night God appeared to Solomon, and said to him, "Ask! What shall I give you?" And Solomon said to God: "You have shown great mercy to David my father, and have made me king in his place." Now, O LORD God, let Your promise to David my father be established, for You have made me king over a people like the dust of the earth in multitude. Now give me wisdom and knowledge, that I may go out and come in before this people; for who can judge this great people of yours?"

Then God said to Solomon: "Because this was in your heart, and you have not asked riches or wealth or honor or the life of your enemies, nor have you asked long life-but have asked wisdom and knowledge for yourself, that you may judge My people over whom I have made you king- wisdom and knowledge are granted to you; and I will give you riches and wealth and honor, such as none of the kings have had who were before you, nor shall any after you have the like.

What motivated Solomon to ask for wisdom? Proverbs 4:3-7, written by Solomon holds the answer.

When I was my father's son, Tender and the only one in the sight of my mother, He also taught me, and said to me: "Let your heart retain my words; Keep my commands, and live. Get wisdom! Get understanding! Do not forget, nor turn away from the words of my mouth. Do not forsake her, and she will preserve you; Love her, and she will keep you. Wisdom is the principal thing; Therefore get wisdom. And in all your getting, get understanding."

Solomon asked for wisdom because his father had imprinted the need for it deep in his heart as a young boy. David probably reinforced his instruction daily, "get wisdom and with it, understanding." Then, when God asked the question, I imagine Solomon's response took little thought. From the abundance of his heart his mouth spoke. Luke 6:45 says, *"A good man out of the good treasure of his heart brings forth good; and an evil man out of the evil treasure of his heart brings forth evil. For out of the abundance of the heart his mouth speaks."*

This is what Sarah did. When she learned the truth of Jeff #1's past, she spoke from the conviction of her heart, without hesitation. She had an image on the inside of what kind of man her husband would be, and Jeff #1 did not fulfill that. Both of her parents had helped her develop that image and she was drawing on that to make her decision. This was demonstrated even further in the story of a conversation she had with her grandfather after becoming engaged to Jeff #2.

The Power of Influence

Sarah had always felt distant from her grandfather. He had walked away from his marriage and the rest of the family before she was born while her dad was serving in Viet Nam. He had made little effort to stay in contact with her dad and even less with his grandchildren. But to her surprise, he called her.

"I'll be in town this weekend and wanted to stop by and see my granddaughter. Would that be OK?" he asked. His leaving had hurt a lot of people but she could sense his desire to begin mending fences. Although she hardly knew him, she graciously agreed on a time to meet.

He was warm and friendly and obviously searching for something to talk about. With little in common, her fiancé soon became the subject of the conversation. She had heard the question before.

"Are you sure he's the right man?"

"Yes, I love him and Dad believes he's the one."

"Well, that's good, but it's not up to your dad, it's up to you."

Leaning forward she looked him straight in the eyes. "Granddad, it was my decision, but I would never marry anyone my father and mother didn't approve of." He was surprised by her strong response and quickly changed the direction of the conversation.

For some it might be hard to imagine this kind of interaction between father and daughter. After all, this was an independent 22-year-old woman who was very capable of making her own decisions. Why was Sarah so quick to shut the door on Jeff #1, and what right did her father have to interfere and insist on questioning the man she was seeing? If you are asking yourself these questions, then you may not yet fully understand the responsibilities of a father and a mother, the power they have to influence, guide, and protect.

The influence parents have in an adult child's life doesn't happen automatically. It is created over a lifetime of love and sacrifice demonstrated through words, actions, and deeds.

The influence parents have in an adult child's life doesn't happen automatically. It is created over a lifetime of love and sacrifice demonstrated through words, actions, and deeds.

Sarah felt great confidence and security knowing her parents approved of Jeff #2. It gave her the freedom to give her whole heart to Jeff #2. She had lived with two good examples and had watched how her father treated her mother. Her dad was certainly not a perfect husband, even Sarah could see that, but he obviously loved her mom and had given her the freedom to be who and what she was created to be. This all contributed to the image of her future husband in her heart. She wasn't expecting perfection in a man, but on issues of character, she would not compromise.

Unfortunately, not every young woman has the advantage of a good example. Recently, the mother of a beautiful teenage girl approached me with tears in her eyes. "Jim, have you got a few minutes? I need to talk to someone." She was heartbroken because she had just learned that her daughter had been sending nude pictures of herself to a boyfriend via her cell phone. Sadly, "sexting" is becoming common place in our schools today, with some of the participants as young as eleven and twelve. "What should I do?" she asked.

It wasn't hard to discern the desperation and sense of helplessness she was feeling. But her question doesn't have a simple answer. What she had discovered was only a symptom of a bigger problem, the seeds of which had been planted years earlier. They were growing unseen beneath the surface long before the behavior ever manifested.

As this mother continued to tell her story, the picture became clear. Her husband had recently ended an affair with a younger woman not much older than their daughter. The marriage was in crisis. Their daughter needed the love and affection of her father, but because of his infidelity and the accompanying lustful thoughts, he could not bring himself to give her a much needed hug without feeling guilty. The end result was a girl seeking affection in all the wrong places. She was compromising her virtue in a desperate attempt to gain what she perceived as love and acceptance.

But, praise God, in this case there was a determined mother who would not allow this to happen. I was happy to learn later that this mother's early discovery of the situation, along with her prayerful and loving intervention, was enough to turn her daughter around.

Our daughters want to be loved and feel safe. They need the affectionate love of their fathers and the security that they provide. When that love and security is missing in the home, many look to others to fill those needs. Mark understood that and for the twenty-one years that Sarah lived at home he had been the man in her life.

We must teach our daughters that there are many unprincipled young men who will gladly offer affection and the promise of security in the hope of intimacy. But it's only an illusion that will end in disaster leaving them feeling empty and worthless. They need to know that men may enjoy the pleasures of intimacy without commitment, but they will never truly respect a woman of compromise.

We must teach our sons to respect and honor women in word and deed. Without respect and honor, there is only lust and abuse. We must say to our sons: "You have no right to intimacy until you have made a lifetime commitment through marriage." It's these kinds of messages, delivered at the right time, that will shape the hearts of our children. When they are spoken in love without judgment and condemnation, they will be welcomed like a cool breeze on a warm day, and we will have helped our children to establish the boundaries in their hearts that will affect their behavior throughout their lives.

Contending for the Heart

Discussions Questions
Chapter 6
The Power of Influence

1. What are your hopes and expectations for your child?

2. Have any of your hopes and expectations for them been realized?

3. In what ways can you encourage your children to wait for God's best for their lives?

4. What are you imprinting in the heart of your child about the nature God? Are you teaching your child about the plans He has for his or her life?

5. What images about your child's future spouse, career choice, and purpose are you helping your child to develop?

6. Can you recall a time(s) when you used raw determination to see your child through a personal struggle?

7. Is your child more influenced by you or the world in regards to intimacy and compromise? What can you do at this point in your child's life to win his or her heart?

8. Is your home an environment where your children feel loved, cared for, and safe?

Chapter 7

——◆━◆◆◆━◆——

It's Never Too Late

O n the first Thursday of each month Keith attended the board meeting of his church. He had served as a board member for the last eight years, but this year he was the acting chairman. He looked forward to the added responsibility, especially since it gave him the power to set the agenda.

The meetings usually ran longer with him at the helm, and this one was no exception. It was nearly 11:00 PM by the time he got home. His wife, Michelle, was sitting quietly at the kitchen table with a cup of tea and a box of tissue; it was obvious she had been crying.

"What's wrong?" Keith asked.

"David locked himself in his room again. He's

been in there since dinner, his music is blaring, and he won't answer when I knock on the door."

"Well, he'll answer me." Keith said as he stormed his way down the hall and up the stairs to David's room. David often reacted this way when he had been grounded. It was his way of getting back at his parents for keeping him in the "cage," as he called it.

"David, you better open up right now! Do you hear me?" Keith shouted, pounding the door with his fist. "Turn that music down and open this door, now!" There was no response.

Keith headed for the garage. Looking through the tool drawer he grabbed a hammer and a large screwdriver and then ran back upstairs where Michelle was now standing by the door to David's room. "Keith, please calm down," she said.

"I am calm," he roared, "but we're getting in his room one way or another."

He wedged the screwdriver in the door jam and then with three hard blows from the hammer he managed to break the lock and force the door open. To their surprise, David was nowhere to be found. The bedroom window was wide open and the screen which had been removed was leaning against the wall.

The room was cold, and it was obvious that he had made his escape hours earlier.

"That's it, Michelle," Keith blurted. "If he's going to treat us like this, then as far as I am concerned he can find somewhere else to live."

"You don't really mean that, Keith," she said, with tears streaming down her cheeks.

"Yes I do," he said. "We can't live like this anymore!"

David, once a well behaved little boy, was now out of control. His strong academic achievements in middle school and junior high had been replaced with failing grades in three of his high school classes. Although David was seventeen, he wasn't driving yet. His father had said that he would not allow him to get a driver's license until he could show that he deserved it. This was just one more item in a long string of performance-based requirements that David felt he could never reach, so he quit trying. He was in a downward spiral, gradually becoming more self-absorbed, angry, and defiant toward anyone in authority, especially his father.

Keith closed the window and then the two of them walked slowly down the stairs to the living room and sat next to each other on the sofa. "I just don't understand," Michelle said. "What have we done wrong?"

Before Keith could answer, the phone rang.

"Hello?"

"Hello, this is Sergeant Jefferson. Is this Mr. Keith Wilson?"

"Yes."

"Do you have a son by the name of David Aaron Wilson?"

"Yes, what's wrong?"

"We have your son here at the police station. He's been arrested for disorderly conduct and underage drinking. Other than being very drunk, he seems OK. But since he's a minor, you'll need to come down to the station."

"I'll get there as soon as I can. It will probably take about twenty minutes."

"No problem," said the officer. "He's not going anywhere."

Keith hung up the phone and looked at Michelle.

"What's happened, what's wrong?" she asked.

"David's been arrested. He's all right, but apparently drunk. They want me to come to the station. " Keith grabbed his coat and headed out the door. "I knew something like this was going to happen."

He had managed to contain his emotions for Michelle's sake, but now that he was alone in the car his anger exploded, and he hit the steering wheel again and again with the palm of his hand. "I can't believe this is happening to us," he shouted. He looked up at the sky and pointed his finger, "You know we don't deserve this."

Keith had accepted Jesus as his savior when he was thirteen and considered himself to be a good Christian. He took pride in the fact that he could practically count on one hand the number of times he had missed a Sunday service. For him, it was all about keeping the rules and living up to the standard of behavior that he believed God expected.

He strictly applied the same standards in raising David. Like many parents, Keith made the mistake of measuring his success by his child's behavior. If David behaved well, then he was a good father, if not then he was a poor father. As logical as that seemed to him, it became a recipe for the inevitable disaster in their family.

At the station, Sergeant Jefferson explained the situation. "We have your son in the holding tank. We can release him into your custody or keep him here for the night. In either case, he will have to appear in front of the judge tomorrow morning, and you'll need to be there."

"How drunk is he?" Keith asked.

"Well, I don't think he can stand on his own," said the sergeant.

"If that's the case, I'll leave him here with you. Maybe a night in jail will put the fear of God in him."

"Do you want to talk to him?" the sergeant asked.

"No. In his condition, what's the point?"

"OK, you can pick him up in the morning any time after 8:00 a.m. Then you will need to be in County Courtroom 235, by 9:00 a.m., Mr. Wilson. The judge will want to talk with both of you."

"We'll be there," Keith said.

For Keith, this was the ultimate embarrassment. It could never be kept quiet in this small Texas town where everyone knows everyone else's business. Keith had worked hard to become successful and was always careful to protect his good name and reputation. He and Michelle were well known and respected in their community, and now he believed their good name was in jeopardy. The humiliation they had faced because of David's previous behavior was about to get worse and Keith knew it.

On the drive home, he found himself obsessed with thoughts about what people might be saying at church on Sunday: "Did you hear about Keith's son? Yeah, I guess Keith is not as good a father as he wanted everyone to believe." Then he thought, *What will I tell people? How will I ever explain this?*

A few blocks from home, he turned into a deserted mall parking lot to stop for a moment and think. Sitting there quietly, he decided to pray. "Heavenly Father, why are You letting this happen? Michelle and I have been good parents. We've always taken our children to church. We made them memorize Bible verses when they were little and if they needed a spanking we gave them one, just like your Word teaches. Your Word says that if we bring them up in the ways of the Lord, then when they are old they will not depart. If that is true, why is this happening?"

Keith sat there quietly thinking about what he had just prayed. It sounded more like an attempt at vindication than a prayer, even to him. *What's wrong with me?* he thought. *My son is in trouble and all I seem to be worried about is what people will think of me. Have I really become that selfish?*

Keith leaned forward and rested his head against his hands on the steering wheel. His head spun as he realized that his lifelong attempt to "keep the rules and live a good life" had failed. *I've earned the respect of my friends but I'm losing my son,* he thought. *What have I done?* He had never felt so alone, empty, and helpless. In that dark deserted parking lot he finally came to the end of himself. The dam of self-righteousness that had been holding back the love of God all his life collapsed, and he cried uncontrollably.

Nearly half an hour passed before he regained enough composure to whisper these desperate and heartfelt words, "Lord, I'm so sorry. What should I do?" In the next few moments, he was overwhelmed with the presence of God's love. He didn't feel judged or condemned, but accepted and forgiven. It was like nothing he had ever experienced and for the first time in his life he realized that God loved him—unconditionally.

He had been parked there for over an hour when his cell phone rang. It was Michelle. "You've been gone a long time. Is everything all right?"

"Yes, more than all right," he replied. "I'll be home in a few minutes and tell you what's happened."

When he arrived back at the house, Michelle was standing by the door. She knew by the tone of his voice on the phone that something was radically different.

"We'd better sit down," he said, "I have a lot to tell you." Tears filled his eyes as he told her the story. Then he took Michelle's hand and looked her in the eyes, "I've been so wrong, I'm so sorry." It was the first time in their twenty-one years of marriage that Michelle had ever seen him cry. "I can't explain it, but something has changed." Then he smiled, "I know what we are supposed to do about David. God showed me."

The next morning, Keith arrived at the station early. The police released David and they walked the three blocks to the courthouse together in near silence. All Keith said was, "I love you, David, and I'm here for you." David said nothing.

Since this was his first arrest, the judge released David into his father's custody with a strong warning:

"If I ever see you in my courtroom again, it won't go this easy. Do you understand me, son?"

"Yes, sir," David replied.

They left the courtroom and headed home. It was obvious to Keith that David was in no mood for conversation. In the past, that would not have mattered. The twenty minute drive home would have begun with a lecture and ended in an argument. But this time, Keith did not repeat that mistake.

After dinner, Keith took Michelle to the den and closed the doors. "There is something about last night in the parking lot I haven't told you yet. Michelle, I think we are supposed to buy David a pickup. How would you feel about that?"

"How do I feel about that?" she said. "Let's go right now before you change your mind!"

"I don't think the dealerships are open this late," Keith said with a chuckle. "Tomorrow is Saturday; let's go first thing."

The next morning, Keith and Michelle headed for the dealership. After an hour or two of looking and haggling with the salesman, they settled on a two-year-old, four-wheel-drive pickup.

"David is going to love this!" Michelle said with a big grin.

David was sitting at the dining room table when he saw them pull into the driveway. "I see you got yourself a new pickup," he said sarcastically as they walked in the door.

"It's not mine," Keith replied.

David looked as his father. "Then whose is it?"

"It's yours," he said, and threw him the keys.

David's mouth dropped open, "Are you kidding?"

"No, I'm not. It's really yours."

David was stunned, "You said you weren't going to let me drive."

"Yeah, I know what I said. Go on, go take a look at your new pickup."

David headed for the door with Michelle following close behind. His surprise changed to excitement as the reality of having his own truck began to sink in.

Keith watched from the dining room window as his son inspected every detail of his new truck. He stood smiling and thought back to what had happened in the parking lot less than forty-eight hours earlier. In the midst of all the emotion that night, three specific scriptures kept coming to his mind. He had read them many times before, and could quote them convincingly in conversation. But that night in the car he realized that he had never understood them. Those verses became the foundation for the restoration of his relationship with David.

- *And though I bestow all my goods to feed the poor, and though I give my body to be burned, but have not love, it profits me nothing.*
  (1 Corinthians 13:3)

- *Love never fails.*
  (1 Corinthians 13:8)

- *Or do you despise the riches of His goodness, forbearance, and longsuffering, not knowing that the goodness of God leads you to repentance?*
  (Romans 2:4)

Keith was determined to apply his new understanding of those scriptures to his relationship with David. The pickup was the first demonstration of this unconditional love. It was a gift without any strings attached. David hadn't earned the truck any more than any of us can earn God's favor and blessings. John 10:10 says, *"I have come that they may have life, and that they may have it more abundantly."* Titus 3:4-5 says, *"But when the kindness and the love of God our Savior toward man appeared not by works of righteousness which we have done, but according to His mercy He saved us."*

David and Michelle were now sitting in the front seat of the pickup talking. Keith walked outside to join them. It was obvious that David was happy but he couldn't bring himself to say thank you to either of his parents. "Wow, nice truck," would have to do for now. The deep hurts inside could not be resolved with a gift, but it was a beginning.

David didn't change immediately, but Keith loved him, helped when he could, and refused to condemn or judge. He was often frustrated when his efforts seemed to be ineffective but he was determined to stay the course no matter the personal cost.

As Keith's heart changed, not only did it affect his relationship within his family, but with others around him as well. People, who he assumed were mocking him for his failure as a father, began to offer their help. "If David needs a job, I have an opening at my store," one fellow board member said. Another friend who was a high school teacher offered to tutor David in the evenings or on weekends. Keith's change of heart had opened the door to God's blessings.

One evening about a year later, David arrived home with a young woman they had never met. "Hi Dad, hi Mom," he said. Then without another preliminary remark, "I want you to meet Angel, my wife. The Justice of the Peace married us on Monday. We have an apartment and will be living there from now on."

Michelle didn't hesitate a second. She walked up to Angel, gave her a hug and said, "Welcome to the family."

It took Keith a few seconds to wrap his mind around what he had just heard, but he soon followed Michelle's lead, "Yes, welcome to the family."

For the next couple of hours Keith and Michelle listened as David and Angel told their story. They had been seeing each other for about six months and as they described it, had fallen madly in love. They had decided to get married as soon as they were the age at which they no longer needed legal permission from their parents. They were married on the day Angel turned eighteen.

"I'm going up to get some of my clothes," David said as he headed for his room.

"I'll come with you," Keith said. He followed him to his room and then sat on the edge of the bed as David gathered his belongings. "David, may I ask you a question?"

"Sure."

"Why didn't you tell me you were thinking about getting married?"

"That's easy. I knew you wouldn't approve."

Keith thought for a minute and then responded, "You know what David? You're right, and I'm sorry."

Keith was learning to love the people around him instead of trying to control them. And the fruit of that was beginning to manifest in his relationship with David. By the time their granddaughter was born eleven months later, the wounds were healing and they were becoming friends.

Several years later, Keith asked David, "What do you think it was that caused you to be so rebellious when you were a teenager?"

David's answer surprised him. "You know what Dad, I haven't got a clue. I guess I just wasn't happy. Why, what do think it was?"

"David, I'm convinced it was my fault. I think it's time I tell you the story of what happened to me that night you were arrested." As Keith recalled the events of that night he could not hold back the tears. When he finished, he looked David in the eyes, "I'm sorry I caused you so much pain. Will you forgive me?"

"It's OK Dad, I already have."

Unlike the parents in the stories of the previous chapters, Keith and Michelle had never really understood that God loved them unconditionally. Keith had established a standard for the behavior of his children and he was determined they would live up to it. When David was little, Keith spanked him, but it was more about punishment than correction. He achieved the desired change in behavior, but never considered what was happening in David's heart.

When David was older, Keith continued to use external pressures in an attempt to force compliance with his rules. He would ground him, take away computer privileges, or prevent him from participating in sports or special events with his friends. In time these methods no longer worked—David was out of control and there was nothing they could do.

The idea of winning David's heart had never crossed Keith's mind. Keith had been living a rigid, performance-based life as an adult. He was unable to bring his son to a place he had never gone himself. Everything changed that night in the empty parking lot when selfishness finally gave way to the love and grace of God. Having finally understood that he himself was forgiven and accepted by God, he could now love David and everyone else in the same way.

Discussions Questions
Chapter 7
It's Never Too Late

1. Have you fallen into the trap of measuring your success by your child's behavior? If so, are you willing to let go of the determination to keep that standard of behavior intact?

2. What verses in scripture can you apply to your relationship with your spouse and children? Are you committed and determined to apply them?

3. Are there areas of your heart that have become hardened and are holding back the love of God? If so, what do you think they are and will you allow the Holy Spirit to heal them?

4. What standards of behavior have you set that may be hard for your children to live up to?

5. What pressures and extern means are you using in an attempt to make your child comply with your rules? Do you believe there is a place for these even with your teens, (for example, grounding, revoking phone or computer privileges, not allowing your child to see friends, etc.)?

6. What do you think it means to be forgiven and accepted by God?

7. How do you think your understanding of God's love for you influences the way you parent?

Chapter 8

---◆━×━◆---

Food For Thought

Forgive and Forget

If you want the transition from law to grace to be graceful for your children, then remember to forgive and forget. Grace is a difficult concept for them to learn if they are constantly reminded of their mistakes. Give your children a clean slate every day no matter how many times they commit the same offense. God does. Jeremiah 31:34 says in part, *"For I will forgive their iniquity and their sin I will remember no more."*

If you remind your children of their failures enough, they will begin to identify with them. My wife, Shirley, and I made it a policy to never use words that link bad behavior to our children's identity. If they acted foolishly, we didn't call them foolish. If they stole something, we didn't call them a thief. If they told a lie, we didn't call them a liar. We first dealt with the behavior in a way that would affect the heart and then we helped them define who they really were by declaring, "You are a son or a daughter of God. You're wise, truthful, honest, and full of the Holy Spirit."

Love them with all your heart and be willing to admit your mistakes to them. Ask for their forgiveness when you're wrong and then watch their love and respect for you grow.

While you're forgiving and forgetting your children's failures, remember to forgive yourself as well. All parents feel like they have made many mistakes in raising their children. But children are more resilient and forgiving than you may think. Love them with all your heart and be willing to admit your mistakes to them. Ask for their forgiveness when you're wrong and then watch their love and respect for you grow. Through your example of humility they will learn to forgive others, forgive themselves, and most importantly to accept the forgiveness of God in their lives.

The Heart is a Canvas

Raising children is not a science or a mathematical equation to be solved. There are no secret formulas or seven step plans that can guarantee success. Raising children is an art and their heart is the canvas. In one hand, parents hold the brush of love and responsibility and in the other, a palette of words, actions, and deeds. With every stroke parents are painting an indelible image on the canvas of their child's heart. It's an image of who God is and how their children will see themselves in relationship to Him. It's that image that will inevitably determine the boundaries of their child's behavior. It doesn't require parents to have the skill of a Picasso or Rembrandt. It only requires a heart of love and willingness to keep painting in spite of the many mistakes.

And God, who knew our children before they were in their mother's womb (Jeremiah 1:5), made no mistake when he chose you to shape the heart of your unique child.

Keep this in mind, the image can never be clearly seen in the process of painting. But when it's complete and you take a few steps back, the true beauty of the image is revealed.

Every child, parent, and family has its own unique characteristics. The chemistry and make-up within a marriage is a blend of personality, gifts and talents that cannot be duplicated. Each child conceived through that marriage has been fearfully and wonderfully made by God; (Psalms 139:14) no two are ever alike. Together the parents and their children form a family like no other. And God, who knew our children before they were in their mother's womb (Jeremiah 1:5), made no mistake when he chose you to shape the heart of your unique child.

God has literally placed His faith in parents. He expects them to mold the heart and lead their children to eternal life with Jesus. However, He does not leave us without divine help. He works with us through the Holy Spirit who the Bible says will lead us into all truth, teach us all things, show us things to come and bring to our remembrance the things that Jesus has said (John 14:26 & 16:13). Every parent needs a friend like Him, the One who holds the answers.

Strongholds

A stronghold is a well defended and fortified position which is difficult to penetrate. Every time you allow bad behavior of any kind, word or deed, to go unchecked without bringing about a change of heart, you are adding fortifications to a stronghold.

The next time the behavior occurs it will become even more difficult to correct.

When our children were small, Shirley and I made the decision that nothing would be allowed to slide. Bad behavior would be addressed immediately unless circumstances would not allow it. By dealing with disobedience immediately and following through to repentance and reconciliation, strongholds never developed in their hearts. We also made the decision that we would do our best not to create strongholds with our words. For example, words of condemnation create strongholds of self-judgment and guilt. Words of criticism destroy initiative and creativity which can create a stronghold of failure. Words of complaint magnify the problems rather than emphasizing the solutions. Many of the bad decisions made by adults are rooted in the strongholds that were developed when they were children.

2 Corinthians 10:4-5 says, *"For the weapons of our warfare are not carnal but mighty in God for pulling down strongholds, casting down arguments and every high thing that exalts itself against the knowledge of God, bringing every thought into captivity to the obedience of Christ."*

Shelter and Protect

When we decided to enroll our children in a private Christian school one of the common criticisms we heard was, "Don't you think you should expose your children to the real world? After all, they're going to have to live there, aren't they?"

To that I answered, "I would no more expose my kids to the evil influences of this world unprepared than I would throw them into the deep end of a swimming pool without first teaching them to swim."

By any and all means protect your children in spirit, soul and body. Allow them to keep their innocence for as long as possible. There is more than enough time for them to learn of the evil and degradation of man. Spend your time filling their minds with the knowledge of God. If you'll do that, evil will stand out to them like an ink spot on a white shirt.

> *"I would no more expose my kids to the evil influences of this world unprepared than I would throw them into the deep end of a swimming pool without first teaching them to swim."*

Be especially careful about who you allow to speak into the lives of your children and what material you allow them to read and view. These are difficult to control in the Information Age, but it can be done. Philippians 4:8 says,

> *Finally, brethren, whatever things are true, whatever things are noble, whatever things are just, whatever things are pure, whatever things are lovely, whatever things are of good report, if there is any virtue and if there is anything praiseworthy—meditate on these things.*

Going It Alone

If you've ever felt like you're standing alone as the single sane voice in the lives of your children, you just might be right. The day has long since passed when you could depend on the teacher, the Cub Scout leader, the soccer coach, or even the youth leader to support you in your efforts to instill values in your kids.

When I was a child in the late 1950's, my parents never worried about the kinds of issues young parents face today. People were basically dependable and moral. Even if the equipment had been available, they could not have imagined the need to video tape the baby sitter. Nor did they consider the possibility that someone in authority might have a secret perverted agenda. But times have changed, and as parents, we must be vigilant and involved in every aspect of our children's lives, taking nothing for granted. Take courage, for the Bible says that where sin abounds grace much more abounds (Romans 5:20). Make sure you stay tuned to the Holy Spirit who can warn you of impending danger.

When I was a young boy, my mother prevented what could have been a terrible disaster by listening to that voice. I was eight or nine at the time, playing at a friend's house across the street. She said that while she was washing the clothes, she felt a sudden urgency to check on me. She walked across the street to the backyard where several of us boys were playing. We were just about to light a match to the pile of wood we had just doused with gasoline when she showed up. Several of us had spilled gas on our clothes and the gas can was sitting next to the woodpile. Who knows what might have happened without her intervention? That was the Holy Spirit leading her to protect me.

This is very important: train your children to listen for that still small voice as well. All children can hear it, they just need to practice. It's one of the ways that He guards and keeps us safe.

Cares Of Life

All of us have at one time or another found ourselves consumed by the cares of life. It can happen when we become focused on basic needs in times of financial stress. Or maybe we have allowed ourselves to become driven by ambition to build our career and reach our goals. Or we might find ourselves involved in a myriad of activities which are good but not necessarily important. Providing a home, building a career, and being involved in things like exercise programs, personal development, or volunteer work are all good, but as we work our way through these cares of life, we cannot forget that our children still need our love and attention.

Contending for the heart of your child requires focus. Parents need to make sure that parenting stays at the top of the priority list and that important daily opportunities to influence their children are not lost in the demands of life.

Billy Graham, a wise minister, once wrote this: "I have sat by the bedside of many powerful and successful men in the very last days of their lives. I asked them, 'What would you do differently if you could live your life again?' Not one ever said, 'I would build another business, earn another million, or even do more to help change the world.' Without exception, they all said they would spend more time with their family at the expense of their personal ambitions."

But we cannot allow ourselves to become so involved in good things that we sacrifice the essential: a rich and loving relationship with our children.

Keep Your Cares to Yourself

Be careful what you communicate to your children in the midst of a problem. I once heard a father say to his child, "No, you can't have those tennis shoes. My boss said he might have to lay me off and we need the money. Quit asking me for things." His statement may have been true, but with that comment he transferred the weight of his fears to his child.

This applies to marriage problems as well. More than one child has felt they are the cause of Mom and Dad's arguments. It's a burden they should never have to bear. Keep your disagreements private. Let your children be children, keep them free of your worries and problems. They will have their own dragons to slay when they're adults.

Slow Down

Many parents believe they're failing if their child is not enrolled in a long list of special programs to develop their skills and talents. In families with several children, the schedules can become so demanding that Moms are often reduced to transportation and activity directors. The children become so entertainment and activity minded, they can hardly sit for an hour to concentrate on a task or read a book. What they are trying to accomplish isn't wrong, it's good. But we cannot allow ourselves to become so involved in good things that we sacrifice the essential: a rich and loving relationship with our children.

Love and Sacrifice

Love and sacrifice go together—they're inseparable. The greater our sacrifice for someone, the more our love for that person grows. It's true with our spouse, it's true with our children, and it's true with a friend. This is an important lesson that our children need to learn. The love they have for Jesus and for people will, at least in part, be proportionate to the sacrifices they make for them.

Young people are looking for purpose and meaning more than at any other time in history. They have cell phones, computers, GPS locators, and career counselors, yet no idea where they're going. So, while they are still at home, place them in circumstances which will

The greater our sacrifice for someone, the more our love for that person grows.

allow them to experience the joy of giving their time, resources, and efforts to help others. Teach your kids that life is not all about them. Teach them to be givers.

The world is saying *Get it, can it, and then sit on the can. God is saying Give it, use it, release it, and I'll bless you.*

Matthew 20: 26-28 says, *"Yet it shall not be so among you; but whoever desires to become great among you, let him become your servant. And whoever desires to be first among you, let him be your slave— just as the Son of Man did not come to be served, but to serve, and to give His life a ransom for many."*

II Corinthians 5:15 says, *"and He died for all, that those who live should live no longer for themselves, but for Him who died for them and rose again."*

Matthew 6:33 counsels us to, *"seek first the kingdom of God and His righteousness, and all these things shall be added unto you."*

Luke 6: 38 says, *"Give, and it will be given to you: good measure pressed down, shaken together, and running over will be put into your bosom. For with the same measure that you use it will be measured back to you."*

James 4: 10 says, *"Humble yourself in the sight of the Lord, and He will lift you up."*

Is Consequence a Good Teacher?

Should children learn that the gas flames on the stove are hot by the parents allowing them to place a hand in the fire? The answer is an obvious "no." While children are young, parents can apply a carefully controlled short term consequence like a spanking. It piques the child's attention and allows the parent to teach the lesson without any harm. In the process children also learn to respond to their parent's words of protection.

This is part of moving your children out from under the law into grace. Your words and the Word of God will establish in their hearts boundaries of behavior that serve to protect them. These boundaries are critically important as our children get older because we no longer have control of the consequences. For example, a one-time experimentation with methamphetamines could literally destroy a young person's mind or end their life. No good lessons are learned from tragedies like this; it only leaves regret and sorrow for everyone.

2 Corinthians 7:8-10 says,

For even if I made you sorry with my letter, I do not regret it; though I did regret it. For I perceive that the same epistle made you sorry, though only for a while. Now I rejoice, not that you were made sorry, but that your sorrow led to repentance. For you were made sorry in a godly manner, that you might suffer loss from us in nothing. For godly sorrow produces repentance leading to salvation, not to be regretted; but the sorrow of the world produces death.

Food for Thought

I encourage you to do everything you can to stand between your child and behaviors that could bring about a devastating consequence. When our children were teenagers, if one of them said they would be attending a party at a friend's house chaperoned by the parents, I took the time to drive across town and make an unexpected visit to see for myself. I didn't do it every time, but they knew the possibility always existed.

My son once asked, "Dad, don't you trust me?" I answered him this way: "It's not that I don't trust you, I just don't trust the flesh. Any one of us can have a weak moment and then do something we would regret the rest of our life. I just want to give you one more reason to do the right thing." Checking on them was not an act of distrust but one of love and they knew it. It was all preparation for the time there would no longer be any parental control.

Discussions Questions
Chapter 8
Food For Thought

1. How easy or difficult is it for you to forgive and forget?

2. Are you able to give your child a clean slate every day?

3. Are you using words that link bad behavior to your child's identity?

4. Is there any area of your child's life where you have a tendency to remind him or her of past failures?

5. Are your children hearing words of condemnation or encouragement, criticism or praise, complaint or gratitude?

6. What decisions have you made about the words and behavior that will be allowed in your home?

7. What worldly influences are being allowed? Ask the Holy Spirit to warn you of any impending danger.

8. Does your child know the still small voice of God? If not, how can you help your child learn to hear it?

9. What can you do to fill your child's mind with the knowledge of God?

10. Are you aware of comments you have made in the midst of difficulties that have transferred the weight of your fears to your child?

11. How can you teach your children the joy of giving their time, resources, and efforts to help others? How do you think it helps a child to know that life isn't all about him or her?

12. What are you doing to ensure that parenting stays at the top of your priority list, and that the demands of life aren't stealing away daily opportunities to influence the heart of your child?

Contending for the heart of your family / child requires determination, focus and a willingness to humble yourself and to lay down the cares of your life and this world. Ask the Holy Spirit to reveal what is in your own heart regarding strongholds, beliefs, and myths about raising children. Depend on Him to change your hearts and adjust your attitudes.

Many have felt that it was too late to start this process. Others felt hopeless, stuck, powerless, or overwhelmed. It's never too late so never give up. After all, contending for the heart of your family / child is a reasonable service to each other and to future generations. And one day, if you will weary not in well doing, your children will thank you and become your best friend and confident.

Concluding Thoughts

As Shirley and I reminisce about the wonderful years we had with our children, we feel a hint of loss. The joy we experienced on our journey far exceeded any momentary pain we might have felt while raising them. And now, we've been rewarded with a tremendous son-in-law, a wonderful daughter-in-law and so many grandchildren that Grandpa can't keep the birthdays straight and Grandma is always en route to or from the Baby Gap.

You will always be their parent and they will always be your children. Personally, I was surprised to discover, after our children were married and having babies of their own, that I continued to feel responsible. It was then I realized our journey with them was not going to end until we leave this earth. Our relationship with them has certainly changed. It has progressed from parent and authority to friend and confidant. And yet, when serious situations arise they still long for the reassurance and security that we can give.

God places children in our custody for what now seems to me, far too short a time. If you're a parent or just thinking about becoming one, be sure and make every day with them count. Never allow yourself to think that you have plenty of time - in the blink of an eye they'll be grown. Enjoy this amazing journey with your children; they are truly a gift and a blessing from the Lord.

Receive Jesus as Your Savior

Praying with your children to receive Jesus Christ as their Lord and Savior is a great privilege and the most important responsibility you will ever fulfill as a parent. God's Word promises,

"If you confess with your mouth the Lord Jesus and believe in your heart that God has raised Him from the dead, you will be saved. For with the heart one believes unto righteousness, and with the mouth confession is made unto salvation." (Rom. 10:9–10,13)

By His grace, God has already done everything to provide salvation. Your part is simply to help your children understand and then believe and receive.

Pray this prayer and have your child repeat it: "Jesus, I believe in my heart that you died for my sins and that God raised You from the dead. I confess that You are my Lord and Savior. By faith in Your Word, I receive salvation now. Thank You for saving me!"

Receive the Holy Spirit

Now that your children have received Jesus, their loving heavenly Father wants to give them the supernatural power needed to live their new life.

"For everyone who asks receives, and he who seeks finds, and to him who knocks it will be opened... If you then, being evil, know how to give good gifts to your children, how much more will your heavenly Father give the Holy Spirit to those who ask Him!"

(Luke 11:10,13)

Pray this prayer with your children: "Father, I recognize my need for Your power to live this new life. Please fill me with Your Holy Spirit. By faith, I receive it right now! Thank You for baptizing me. Holy Spirit, You are welcome in my life."

Congratulations! Now you're filled with God's supernatural power. Some syllables from a language you don't recognize will rise up from your heart to your mouth. (See 1 Cor. 14:14.) As you speak them out loud by faith, you're releasing God's power from within and building yourself up in the Spirit. (See v. 4.) You can do this whenever and wherever you like.

It doesn't really matter whether you or your children felt anything or not when they prayed to receive the Lord and His Spirit. If you believed in your heart that you received, then God's Word promises you did.

"Therefore I say unto you, What things so ever ye desire, when ye pray, believe that ye receive them, and ye shall have them" (Mark 11:24)

Please contact Shirley and me and let us know that you've prayed to receive Jesus as your Savior or to be filled with the Holy Spirit. We would like to rejoice with you.

The War Is Over

Peace has been won. The longest conflict in history lasted 4,000 years and ended in a decisive victory nearly 2,000 years ago. Still, many have not yet heard the news and they continue to fight the battle—the battle of sin and judgment.

On the cross Jesus said "It is finished," victory was declared, and reconciliation began. It was the victory promised when Jesus was born and the angels declared, "Glory to God in the highest, and on earth peace, good will toward men" (Luke 2:14). Is this saying Jesus came to create peace among men? If it is, then He has most certainly failed.

The peace He spoke of was not among men, but between God and man. Sin is no longer the issue; the price has been paid once and for all. God sent His only Son to bear our sin, becoming sin itself, and then judged Him without mercy for that sin. Was His sacrifice enough for you? Is God withholding His blessing because of your sin? If you die with an unconfessed sin, would you be lost? The answers in this book will release you from the condemnation of judgment and fear. It will free you to receive the promised blessings of God!

Available at bookstores everywhere
or visit www.harrisonhouse.com

Spirit, Soul & Body

Understanding the relationship of your spirit, soul, and body is foundational to your Christian life. You will never truly know how much God loves you or believe what His Word says about you until you do. In this series, learn how spirit, soul and body are related and how that knowledge will release the life of your spirit into your body and soul. It may even explain why many things are not working the way you had hoped.

Available at bookstores everywhere
or visit www.harrisonhouse.com

The Harrison House Vision

Proclaiming the truth and the power

Of the Gospel of Jesus Christ

With excellence;

Challenging Christians to

Live victoriously,

Grow spiritually,

Know God intimately.

Heart of the Family

Vision:

Help establish strong families rooted and grounded in God's Word and bring reconciliation and restoration to those that are struggling and broken.

Mission:

Use every available communication medium to teach the truth of the Bible concerning families. Expose the lies and misconceptions the enemy uses to build walls within the home and destroy relationships. By the power of the Holy Spirit, open the doors to recociliation that will heal marriages and turn the hearts of the children to their parents and the parents to their children. Help families rebuild strong foundations that will withstand the storms of life.

Contact Jim and Shirley Ertel at:

Heart of the Family
P.O. Box 2063
Monument, CO 80132
Website: www.heartofthefamily.org
Email: info@heartofthefamily.org

About the Author

Jim Ertel has been in ministry for twenty five years serving in many capacities. Although he is an ordained minister, he served in partner relations and development for The Christian Broadcasting Network and Oral Roberts University. He is currently the Director of Partner Relations with Andrew Wommack Ministries where he also teaches on family relations at Charis Bible College, founded by Andrew Wommack. Jim and his wife, Shirley, recently celebrated their 40th wedding anniversary. Their son and daughter are both married and between the two have given them six grandchildren. Jim and Shirley have a heart to see families build strong foundations and bring restoration and reconciliation to those who are broken.